SOCIA MEDIA

The Complete Marketing Guide

Sophia Bellamy

Reactive Publishing

CONTENTS

Title Page

Preface   2

Chapter1: The Evolution of Social Media   4

Chapter 2: Content for Social Media   19

Chapter 3: Marketing Strategies   44

Chapter 4: Introduction to Paid Social Media Advertising   63

Chapter 5: Building and Nurturing Online Communities   93

Chapter 6: Social Media Advertising Strategies   111

Chapter 7: Social Listening: Understanding Your Audience   125

Conclusion   130

Additional Resources   132

Step-by-Step Tutorial for Social Media Marketing   135

Copyright Notice

PREFACE

Welcome to the dynamic world of Social Media Marketing. As we navigate the 21st century, the digital landscape continuously evolves, reshaping how businesses communicate, engage, and grow. This book is designed to be your comprehensive guide to mastering the art and science of social media marketing.

In an era where nearly half the global population is active on social media, understanding how to effectively leverage these platforms is crucial for any business aiming for success. From small startups to multinational corporations, social media has become an indispensable tool for reaching and engaging with a diverse audience. Yet, amidst the ever-changing algorithms, trends, and tools, the path to effective social media marketing can often seem daunting.

This book was born out of a passion for helping businesses of all sizes harness the power of social media. Through years of experience in marketing, psychology, and entrepreneurship, I have distilled the essential strategies and insights that can transform your social media presence. Whether you're a seasoned marketer looking to refine your approach or a newcomer eager to make your mark, this book will provide you with the knowledge and tools you need.

We will journey through the foundational principles of social media marketing, explore the nuances of different platforms, and delve into advanced techniques that can set you apart from the competition. You will learn how to create compelling content, engage authentically with your audience, and analyze data to inform your strategies. Additionally, we'll explore case studies and real-world examples to illustrate these concepts in action.

In writing this book, my goal is to equip you with a robust framework for social media marketing that is both practical and adaptable. The strategies outlined here are not mere theories; they are actionable steps that you can implement immediately to see tangible results.

As you embark on this journey, remember that social media marketing is as much an art as it is a science. It requires creativity, persistence, and a deep understanding of your audience. But most importantly, it requires a willingness to experiment, learn, and adapt. The landscape may change, but with the right approach, you can consistently achieve remarkable success.

Thank you for choosing this book as your guide. I am excited to share these insights with you and look forward to seeing the impact you will make in the digital world.

CHAPTER1: THE EVOLUTION OF SOCIAL MEDIA

T he evolution of social media is a fascinating journey that has transformed the way we communicate, share information, and connect with one another. In the early days of the internet, platforms like AOL and MySpace began to pave the way for online communities, offering users the first taste of social interaction in the digital realm. As technology advanced and internet access became more widespread, social media platforms evolved rapidly. Facebook emerged in 2004, revolutionizing the landscape with its innovative approach to connecting people through a more personalized and interactive interface. This was soon followed by the rise of Twitter in 2006, which introduced the concept of microblogging and real-time communication, allowing users to broadcast short messages to a global audience.

The visual-centric Instagram, launched in 2010, further changed the game by emphasizing photo and video sharing, catering to the growing demand for visual content. Meanwhile, LinkedIn established itself as the go-to platform for professional networking, and Pinterest carved out a niche for visual discovery and inspiration. The introduction of Snapchat in

2011 brought ephemeral content to the forefront, changing how users interacted with fleeting moments. TikTok, the latest sensation, has captivated a younger audience with its short-form, highly engaging video content since its global release in 2018. Throughout this evolution, social media has not only adapted to technological advancements but has also influenced and been influenced by cultural shifts, political movements, and global events. Today, social media is an integral part of daily life, shaping how we communicate, market, and consume information, with each platform continuously innovating to meet the ever-changing needs of its users.

1.2 Importance of Social Media in Modern Marketing

In today's digitally connected world, social media has become an indispensable tool for modern marketing. The significance of social media in marketing stems from its unparalleled ability to reach a vast and diverse audience across the globe. Unlike traditional marketing channels, social media platforms offer marketers the opportunity to engage directly with consumers, fostering a sense of community and loyalty that is difficult to achieve through other mediums. With billions of active users on platforms like Facebook, Instagram, Twitter, and LinkedIn, businesses have the potential to amplify their brand message, increase visibility, and attract new customers more effectively than ever before.

One of the key benefits of social media marketing is its cost-effectiveness. Small businesses and startups, which may not have extensive marketing budgets, can leverage social media to compete with larger companies. Furthermore, social media provides valuable insights into consumer behavior and preferences, enabling marketers to tailor their strategies to meet the specific needs and desires of their audience.

Another crucial aspect of social media marketing is its real-time nature. Companies can respond to trends, customer inquiries, and feedback almost instantaneously, fostering a dynamic and interactive relationship with their audience. This immediacy allows for timely promotions, crisis management, and customer support, all of which contribute to a positive brand image and customer satisfaction. Additionally, social media's shareable nature enhances word-of-mouth marketing, as satisfied customers can easily share their positive experiences with their networks, exponentially increasing a brand's reach and credibility.

Moreover, social media platforms are continually evolving, offering new features and tools that marketers can utilize to stay ahead of the competition. From live streaming and stories to augmented reality and shoppable posts, these innovations provide endless opportunities for creativity and engagement.

1.3 Understanding Different Social Media Platforms

Navigating the landscape of social media requires a deep understanding of the unique features and user demographics of each platform. Each social media platform has carved out its niche, catering to different types of content and interactions, making it essential for marketers to tailor their strategies accordingly.

Facebook, the largest social media network, is a versatile platform that supports various content formats, including text, images, videos, and live streams. It is particularly effective for community building and targeted advertising, thanks to its advanced analytics and diverse user base. With over 2.8 billion monthly active users, Facebook offers businesses the opportunity to engage with a wide range of demographics, making it an ideal platform for both B2C and B2B marketing.

Instagram, owned by Facebook, is a visually-driven platform that emphasizes photos and short videos. It has a strong appeal among younger audiences, particularly millennials and Gen Z. Instagram's features, such as Stories, IGTV, and Reels, provide creative avenues for brands to showcase their products, behind-the-scenes content, and user-generated posts. The platform's focus on aesthetics and visual storytelling makes it a powerful tool for brands looking to build a strong, visually cohesive presence.

Twitter, with its fast-paced, real-time nature, is the go-to platform for breaking news, updates, and short-form content. It excels in facilitating direct interaction between brands and consumers, allowing for quick responses to customer queries and feedback. Twitter's use of hashtags enables businesses to join trending conversations and increase their visibility. However, its character limit requires marketers to be concise and impactful in their messaging.

LinkedIn, the premier platform for professional networking, is essential for B2B marketing. It is ideal for sharing industry insights, company updates, and thought leadership content. LinkedIn's audience consists primarily of professionals, making it the perfect place to connect with decision-makers, potential clients, and industry peers. Its advertising options are tailored to target specific job titles, industries, and company sizes, making it highly effective for lead generation and recruitment.

Pinterest, a visual discovery and bookmarking platform, is particularly popular among users seeking inspiration for projects, such as home decor, fashion, and cooking. Brands can leverage Pinterest to drive traffic to their websites through visually appealing pins that link back to their content. The platform's users are predominantly female, making it a valuable channel for brands targeting this demographic.

YouTube, the leading video-sharing platform, offers immense opportunities for content marketing through long-form videos, tutorials, product reviews, and vlogs. Video content on YouTube has a longer lifespan compared to other platforms, providing ongoing value and engagement. YouTube's search engine capabilities also make it a powerful tool for SEO, helping brands increase their visibility and reach a global audience. The platform's diverse user base, spanning various age groups and interests, allows for a wide range of content strategies.

TikTok, the newest major player in the social media arena, has rapidly gained popularity, especially among younger audiences. Its focus on short, engaging videos and its algorithm-driven content discovery make it an excellent platform for virality. Brands can leverage TikTok to showcase their creativity, participate in trends, and connect with a highly engaged community through challenges and user-generated content.

Snapchat, known for its ephemeral content, offers unique opportunities for real-time engagement and interactive experiences. Its features, such as Stories, filters, and lenses, allow brands to create immersive and engaging content that resonates with its primarily young audience. Snapchat's focus on privacy and direct communication makes it a valuable platform for building personal connections with followers.

Understanding the distinct characteristics and user bases of these platforms enables marketers to create tailored strategies that maximize engagement and achieve their marketing goals.

1.4 Setting SMART Goals for Social Media Marketing

Setting SMART goals—Specific, Measurable, Achievable, Relevant, and Time-bound—is crucial for the success of any social media marketing strategy. SMART goals provide a clear roadmap, helping marketers stay focused, track progress, and achieve their desired outcomes.

Specific: The first step in setting SMART goals is to be specific about what you want to achieve. Vague goals like "increase social media presence" are not effective because they lack direction. Instead, define clear objectives such as "gain 1,000 new Instagram followers in three months" or "increase Facebook post engagement by 20% over the next quarter." Specific goals help you understand exactly what you need to do to succeed.

Measurable: To track progress and determine success, your goals must be measurable. This involves setting criteria that allow you to quantify your achievements. For instance, if your goal is to increase website traffic through social media, specify the exact percentage or number of visitors you aim to attract. Tools like Google Analytics and social media insights can help measure your progress. A measurable goal might be "drive 500 additional website visits per month from social media channels."

Achievable: While it's important to set ambitious goals, they should also be realistic and attainable. Setting unattainable goals can lead to frustration and demotivation. Consider your current resources, budget, and the social media landscape when setting your goals. For example, if you're a small business with limited marketing resources, aiming to increase your Twitter followers by 10,000 in a month might be unrealistic. Instead, focus on a more achievable target, such as gaining 500 followers in the same period.

Relevant: Your goals should align with your broader business objectives and be relevant to your overall marketing strategy. Consider how achieving these goals will contribute to your business's success. For example, if your business objective is to increase online sales, a relevant social media goal could be "increase Instagram-driven sales by 15% over the next six months." Ensuring relevance helps keep your efforts aligned with your business priorities.

Time-bound: Finally, setting a deadline for your goals is essential for maintaining focus and urgency. Time-bound goals specify a timeframe within which you aim to achieve your objectives. This could be weekly, monthly, quarterly, or annually, depending on the nature of your goals. For instance, "increase LinkedIn engagement by 30% within the next quarter" gives you a clear deadline to work towards, encouraging consistent effort and timely progress evaluation.

1.5 Key Metrics to Track and Measure Success

Tracking the right metrics is essential for measuring the success of your social media marketing efforts. Here are some of the most important metrics to track:

1. Reach: Reach refers to the total number of unique users who have seen your content. It helps you understand the size of your audience and the potential visibility of your posts. Monitoring reach allows you to gauge the effectiveness of your content distribution and identify which types of content resonate best with your audience.

2. Impressions: Impressions measure how many times your content has been displayed, regardless of whether it was clicked or not. This metric can help you understand the exposure of your posts and the frequency at which your audience is seeing your content. High impressions with low engagement might indicate that your content needs to be more compelling or relevant.

3. Engagement: Engagement metrics include likes, comments, shares, retweets, and other interactions with your content. High engagement indicates that your audience finds your content valuable and interesting. Engagement rates are often expressed as a percentage of total reach or impressions, providing a clearer picture of how well your content is performing.

4. Click-Through Rate (CTR): CTR measures the number of clicks your content receives relative to the number of impressions. It is a critical metric for understanding how effectively your posts are driving traffic to your website or landing pages. A high CTR indicates that your content and call-to-action are compelling and relevant to your audience.

5. Conversion Rate: Conversion rate tracks the percentage of users who take a desired action, such as making a purchase, signing up for a newsletter, or downloading a resource, after clicking on your social media content. This metric is crucial for measuring the ROI of your social media efforts and understanding how well your content is driving business goals.

6. Follower Growth: Tracking the growth of your followers over time helps you understand the long-term impact of your social

media strategy. A steady increase in followers indicates that your content is attracting and retaining an audience. Analyzing follower growth alongside other engagement metrics can provide insights into the overall health of your social media presence.

7. Social Share of Voice (SSoV): SSoV measures your brand's share of conversations within your industry or niche compared to your competitors. It helps you understand how much of the online conversation your brand is capturing and can be a valuable metric for benchmarking your performance against competitors.

8. Sentiment Analysis: Sentiment analysis evaluates the tone and emotion behind social media mentions of your brand. It helps you understand how your audience feels about your brand and content, providing insights into customer satisfaction and brand perception. Positive sentiment indicates a strong brand reputation, while negative sentiment may highlight areas needing improvement.

9. Customer Service Metrics: For brands that use social media for customer service, tracking metrics like response time, resolution time, and customer satisfaction scores is essential. These metrics help you understand how effectively you are addressing customer inquiries and resolving issues, which can impact overall customer satisfaction and loyalty.

10. ROI and Cost Per Result: Calculating the return on investment (ROI) for your social media campaigns involves comparing the revenue generated from social media activities to the total cost of those activities. Additionally, metrics like cost per click (CPC) and cost per acquisition (CPA) help you understand the financial efficiency of your campaigns, allowing you to optimize budget allocation and improve overall performance.

1.6 Identifying and Understanding Your Target Audience

Understanding your target audience is a cornerstone of effective social media marketing.

1. Demographics: Start by analyzing the basic demographic

information of your audience, such as age, gender, location, income level, education, and occupation. This data helps you create a general profile of your typical customer. For instance, if your target audience primarily consists of young adults, your content might be more casual and trendy, whereas an older audience might prefer more informative and respectful tones.

2. Psychographics: Beyond demographics, psychographics delve into the lifestyle, values, interests, and attitudes of your audience. Understanding these aspects helps you connect with your audience on a deeper level. For example, if your target audience values sustainability, creating content that highlights your brand's eco-friendly practices will likely resonate with them.

3. Behavioral Data: Analyzing the online behavior of your audience provides insights into how they interact with social media. Look at the types of content they engage with, the platforms they use most frequently, and their online purchasing habits. This data can help you optimize your content strategy and posting schedule to align with their online activities.

4. Pain Points and Needs: Identify the common challenges and needs of your audience. What problems are they trying to solve? How can your product or service help them? Understanding their pain points allows you to create content that addresses these issues directly, positioning your brand as a valuable resource and solution provider.

5. Customer Feedback and Reviews: Pay attention to what your audience is saying about your brand and products. Customer feedback, reviews, and social media comments can provide valuable insights into what your audience likes, dislikes, and expects from your brand. Use this information to improve your products and tailor your marketing messages.

6. Competitor Analysis: Analyze your competitors to see who they are targeting and how they engage with their audience. This can help you identify potential gaps in the market and opportunities to differentiate your brand. Look at the types of content your

competitors are producing, the platforms they are using, and the engagement levels they are achieving.

7. Social Media Analytics: Utilize the analytics tools provided by social media platforms to gather data on your audience. These tools offer valuable insights into your followers' demographics, behaviors, and engagement patterns. Use this data to refine your audience profiles and adjust your strategies accordingly.

8. Surveys and Polls: Conduct surveys and polls to gather direct feedback from your audience. Asking specific questions about their preferences, interests, and needs can provide detailed insights that help you better understand and serve your audience. Social media platforms offer easy-to-use tools for creating and distributing surveys and polls.

9. Customer Personas: Create detailed customer personas based on the data you have collected. Personas are fictional characters that represent different segments of your audience. Each persona should include demographic information, psychographics, behavior patterns, pain points, and needs. These personas help you visualize your audience and tailor your content and strategies to meet their specific characteristics.

10. Continuous Monitoring and Updating: Audience preferences and behaviors can change over time, so it's essential to continuously monitor and update your understanding of your target audience. Regularly review your social media analytics, customer feedback, and market trends to ensure your strategies remain relevant and effective.

Thoroughly identifying and understanding your target audience, you can create more personalized and impactful social media content, foster stronger connections with your followers, and ultimately drive better marketing results. This targeted approach ensures that your efforts resonate with the right people, enhancing your brand's visibility and effectiveness in the crowded social media landscape.

1.7 Building a Strong Social Media Presence

Building a strong social media presence is essential for establishing your brand's identity, engaging with your audience, and driving business growth. A robust social media presence involves consistent branding, strategic content planning, active engagement, and continuous optimization. Here are key steps to help you build and maintain a powerful social media presence:

1. Define Your Brand Voice and Aesthetic: Start by defining a clear and consistent brand voice and aesthetic that aligns with your brand's identity and resonates with your target audience. Your brand voice encompasses the tone, style, and personality of your communication, while your aesthetic includes visual elements like colors, fonts, and imagery. Consistency in these areas helps build brand recognition and trust.

2. Create a Content Strategy: Develop a comprehensive content strategy that outlines the types of content you will create, the platforms you will use, and the posting frequency. Your strategy should be aligned with your business goals and audience preferences. Include a mix of content types such as educational posts, entertaining videos, behind-the-scenes glimpses, user-generated content, and promotional material.

3. Optimize Your Profiles: Ensure that all your social media profiles are complete, professional, and optimized for search. Use high-quality profile pictures and cover images, write compelling bios that include relevant keywords, and provide accurate contact information. Consistent branding across all profiles reinforces your brand's identity.

4. Engage with Your Audience: Active engagement is crucial for building a loyal and engaged community. Respond promptly to comments, messages, and mentions, and participate in conversations related to your industry. Show appreciation for your followers by acknowledging their feedback and contributions. Engagement fosters a sense of community and builds stronger relationships with your audience.

5. Leverage Hashtags and Keywords: Use relevant hashtags

and keywords to increase the discoverability of your content. Hashtags help categorize your content and make it easier for users interested in specific topics to find you. Research popular and trending hashtags in your industry and incorporate them into your posts strategically.

6. Collaborate with Influencers and Partners: Partnering with influencers and other brands can help expand your reach and credibility. Collaborate with influencers who align with your brand values and have a strong following among your target audience. Influencer partnerships can introduce your brand to new followers and create authentic engagement.

7. Utilize Analytics and Insights: Regularly review your social media analytics to understand what is working and what needs improvement. Analyze metrics such as engagement rates, reach, impressions, and follower growth to gauge the effectiveness of your content and strategies. Use these insights to make data-driven decisions and optimize your social media efforts.

8. Run Social Media Campaigns: Plan and execute social media campaigns to promote specific products, events, or initiatives. Campaigns should have clear objectives, timelines, and measurable outcomes. Use a combination of organic and paid strategies to maximize the impact of your campaigns and reach a broader audience.

9. Invest in Paid Advertising: While organic reach is valuable, paid advertising can significantly boost your visibility and engagement. Social media platforms offer various advertising options, such as sponsored posts, display ads, and video ads. Target your ads based on demographics, interests, and behaviors to ensure they reach the right audience.

10. Stay Current with Trends: Social media is constantly evolving, with new features, trends, and platforms emerging regularly. Stay informed about the latest developments in social media marketing and be willing to experiment with new approaches. Adapting to changes and staying ahead of trends will keep your

brand relevant and competitive.

Building a strong social media presence requires dedication, creativity, and strategic planning.

1.8 Ethical Considerations in Social Media Marketing

Ethical considerations in social media marketing are paramount in maintaining the integrity, trust, and credibility of your brand. In an era where information spreads rapidly and consumers are more informed and discerning than ever, adhering to ethical standards is not just a moral obligation but a strategic necessity. Transparency is one of the fundamental principles of ethical social media marketing. This means being honest about your intentions, disclosing any sponsored content or partnerships, and ensuring that your advertising is truthful and not misleading. Consumers appreciate brands that are open about their practices and can quickly lose trust in those that engage in deceptive tactics.

Respecting user privacy is another critical aspect. With the increasing concern over data security, it is essential to handle personal information with care. This includes obtaining explicit consent before collecting data, being clear about how the data will be used, and ensuring that user data is stored securely. Misuse of personal information can lead to severe repercussions, including legal consequences and damage to your brand's reputation.

Social media marketers must also be mindful of cultural sensitivities and diversity. The global nature of social media means your content can reach a wide and varied audience. It's important to avoid stereotypes, respect cultural differences, and promote inclusivity. This not only helps in creating a positive brand image but also broadens your appeal across different demographics.

Additionally, ethical social media marketing involves responsible use of influencer partnerships. Influencers should genuinely use and endorse the products they promote, and any compensation should be clearly disclosed. Authenticity is key to maintaining the trust of both the influencer's and the brand's audiences.

Avoiding manipulative tactics, such as creating fake reviews or buying followers, is crucial. Such practices may offer short-term gains but can lead to long-term damage to your brand's credibility. Authentic engagement and organic growth are far more sustainable and beneficial in the long run.

Lastly, being responsive and responsible in your communication is vital. This includes addressing customer complaints promptly, admitting mistakes, and taking corrective actions when necessary. Engaging in honest and respectful dialogue with your audience fosters trust and loyalty.

Ethical considerations in social media marketing are about building and maintaining a relationship of trust with your audience.

1.9 The Role of Social Media in Brand Building

Social media has become a cornerstone in the process of brand building, offering unparalleled opportunities for businesses to establish and enhance their brand identity, connect with their audience, and drive engagement. Unlike traditional media, social media provides a dynamic, interactive platform where brands can communicate directly with consumers, creating a more personalized and authentic connection.

One of the key roles of social media in brand building is increasing brand visibility. With billions of users across various platforms, social media allows brands to reach a vast audience. Consistent posting of high-quality content helps maintain a regular presence, ensuring that the brand stays top-of-mind for followers. This visibility is crucial for attracting new customers and retaining existing ones.

Social media also plays a vital role in shaping brand perception. This can be achieved through storytelling, where brands share their journey, successes, and challenges, creating an emotional connection with their audience. Visual content, such as photos and videos, further enhances this narrative by making it more engaging and relatable.

Engagement is another critical aspect of brand building facilitated by social media. Platforms like Facebook, Instagram, and Twitter allow for two-way communication, enabling brands to interact with their audience in real-time. This interaction fosters a sense of community and loyalty among followers. Responding to comments, participating in conversations, and acknowledging user-generated content shows that the brand values its audience, which can significantly strengthen the relationship.

Furthermore, social media serves as a powerful tool for showcasing brand authenticity. In a digital age where consumers are increasingly skeptical of traditional advertising, authenticity can set a brand apart. Sharing behind-the-scenes content, employee stories, and user testimonials can humanize the brand and build trust. Authenticity resonates with audiences, making them more likely to support and advocate for the brand.

Social media also enables brands to leverage influencer partnerships, which can be a highly effective strategy for brand building. Influencers, with their established follower base and trust, can introduce the brand to new audiences and lend credibility. Collaborations with influencers who align with the brand's values and aesthetics can amplify the brand's message and expand its reach.

Additionally, social media analytics provide valuable insights into audience behavior and preferences. This data-driven approach ensures that brand-building efforts are both effective and efficient.

social media plays a multifaceted role in brand building. It enhances brand visibility, shapes perception, fosters engagement, showcases authenticity, leverages influencer partnerships, and provides valuable analytics.

CHAPTER 2: CONTENT FOR SOCIAL MEDIA

Creating diverse and engaging content is fundamental to any successful social media marketing strategy. Different types of content serve various purposes, from building brand awareness to driving engagement and conversions. Understanding the unique characteristics and benefits of each content type can help you effectively communicate with your audience and achieve your marketing goals.

1. Text Posts: Text-based content is straightforward and effective for sharing information, updates, and engaging in conversations with your audience. Whether it's a status update on Facebook, a tweet on Twitter, or a LinkedIn post, text content allows you to communicate clearly and directly. To maximize engagement, ensure your text posts are concise, compelling, and include a clear call-to-action.

2. Images: Visual content is highly engaging and can capture attention more effectively than text alone. High-quality images can be used to showcase products, highlight customer testimonials, share behind-the-scenes glimpses, and convey brand aesthetics. Platforms like Instagram and Pinterest are particularly well-suited for image-based content. Ensure your images are visually appealing, relevant, and optimized for each platform's specifications.

3. Videos: Video content is increasingly popular across all social media platforms. Videos can range from short clips and teasers to long-form content such as tutorials, webinars, and interviews. Videos are effective for storytelling, demonstrating products, and providing value through educational content. Live videos, in particular, offer real-time interaction with your audience, fostering a sense of immediacy and authenticity.

4. Stories: Ephemeral content, such as Stories on Instagram, Facebook, and Snapchat, allows you to share content that disappears after 24 hours. Stories are ideal for sharing quick updates, behind-the-scenes moments, and interactive content like polls and Q&A sessions. Their temporary nature encourages viewers to engage quickly and regularly check back for new updates.

5. Infographics: Infographics combine visuals and text to present complex information in an easy-to-understand format. They are particularly useful for sharing statistics, explaining processes, and providing educational content. Infographics are highly shareable and can help establish your brand as an authority in your industry.

6. User-Generated Content (UGC): Leveraging content created by your customers and followers can enhance authenticity and build community. UGC includes customer reviews, photos, videos, and social media posts that feature your brand. Sharing UGC not only provides social proof but also encourages other followers to create and share their content.

7. Blogs and Articles: Long-form content such as blog posts and articles can be shared on social media to drive traffic to your website and provide in-depth information to your audience. Sharing valuable, informative content helps establish your brand as a thought leader and can improve your search engine rankings.

8. Polls and Surveys: Interactive content like polls and surveys can engage your audience and provide valuable insights into their preferences and opinions. Platforms like Twitter, Instagram

Stories, and Facebook offer built-in tools for creating polls and surveys. This type of content encourages participation and can help you gather feedback for improving your products and services.

9. Contests and Giveaways: Running contests and giveaways on social media can boost engagement, increase your follower count, and generate excitement around your brand. Encourage users to participate by liking, sharing, and commenting on your posts. Clearly outline the rules and prizes, and ensure the contest aligns with your overall marketing goals.

10. Memes and Gifs: Memes and gifs are a fun and relatable way to engage with your audience. They often convey humor and can quickly go viral, increasing your brand's visibility. When using memes and gifs, ensure they align with your brand's tone and are appropriate for your audience.

Experiment with different formats, analyze their performance, and refine your approach to create a dynamic and compelling social media presence.

2.2 Creating Engaging and Shareable Content

Creating engaging and shareable content is the cornerstone of any successful social media strategy. The goal is to capture the attention of your audience, encourage interaction, and motivate them to share your content with their own networks. To achieve this, it's crucial to understand what makes content engaging and how to craft posts that resonate with your audience. At the heart of engaging content is storytelling. People are naturally drawn to stories that evoke emotions, whether it's joy, surprise, empathy, or curiosity. This could involve sharing customer success stories, behind-the-scenes looks at your brand, or personal anecdotes that highlight your company's values and mission.

Visual appeal is another critical component of engaging content. High-quality images, videos, and graphics can significantly enhance the attractiveness of your posts. Visuals not only capture attention but also help convey your message more effectively than text alone. Incorporating visually appealing elements into your content strategy can make your posts more memorable and impactful. Additionally, using tools like Canva or Adobe Spark can help you create professional-looking visuals even if you don't have a graphic design background.

Interactivity is a powerful way to boost engagement. Content that invites users to participate, such as polls, quizzes, challenges, and live Q&A sessions, can significantly increase interaction rates. Interactive posts not only engage your audience but also provide valuable insights into their preferences and opinions. For example, hosting a live Q&A on Instagram or Facebook can allow you to directly address your audience's questions and concerns, fostering a sense of community and trust.

Moreover, understanding your audience's preferences is key to creating content that resonates. Analyzing engagement metrics can reveal which types of posts perform best, allowing you to tailor your content strategy accordingly. For instance, if data shows that your audience prefers video content over static images, you might focus more on producing short, engaging videos. Regularly reviewing these insights helps you stay attuned to your audience's evolving interests and preferences.

Creating shareable content also involves understanding the triggers that motivate people to share. Content that is informative, entertaining, inspirational, or relatable tends to be more shareable. People are more likely to share posts that they find valuable or that reflect their personal beliefs and experiences. Including a clear call-to-action (CTA) in your posts can also encourage sharing. Simple prompts like "Share this with a friend who needs to see this" or "Tag someone who can relate" can effectively drive shares.

Lastly, consistency in posting is vital. A regular posting schedule keeps your brand in your audience's mind and demonstrates reliability. Tools like Buffer or Hootsuite can help you schedule posts in advance, ensuring a steady flow of content. Consistency doesn't just apply to the frequency of posts but also to the quality and tone of your content. Maintaining a consistent voice and visual style helps reinforce your brand identity and fosters trust among your followers.

In summary, creating engaging and shareable content requires a combination of storytelling, visual appeal, interactivity, audience insights, and consistency.

2.3 Visual Content: Photos, Videos, and Graphics

Visual content is a powerful tool in social media marketing, offering a dynamic way to capture attention, convey messages, and engage audiences. Photos, videos, and graphics each play a unique role in enhancing your brand's presence and making your content more appealing and memorable.

Photos are one of the most straightforward and effective forms of visual content. High-quality images can instantly grab attention and communicate your message more effectively than text alone. Whether showcasing your products, sharing customer testimonials, or providing a glimpse behind the scenes, photos can bring your brand to life. To maximize the impact, ensure your photos are well-lit, high resolution, and aligned with your brand's aesthetic. Consistency in style helps reinforce your brand identity and makes your posts instantly recognizable.

Videos have become increasingly important in social media marketing due to their ability to deliver complex messages in an engaging and easily digestible format. They can range from short clips and animated GIFs to longer formats like tutorials, webinars, and vlogs. Videos are particularly effective for storytelling, demonstrating products in action, and providing value through educational content. Live videos add an element of immediacy and authenticity, allowing real-time interaction with your audience. Platforms like Instagram, Facebook, TikTok, and YouTube provide various features for creating and sharing video content, making it easier to reach and engage your audience.

Graphics, including infographics, illustrations, and memes, offer a versatile way to present information visually. Infographics are particularly useful for breaking down complex data into easily understandable visuals, making them ideal for sharing statistics, processes, and educational content. Illustrations and custom graphics can add a unique and creative touch to your social media presence, setting you apart from competitors. Memes, on the other hand, tap into popular culture and trends, providing a fun and relatable way to engage your audience. When using graphics, ensure they are clear, visually appealing, and consistent with your brand's color scheme and style.

Combining different types of visual content can create a more engaging and varied social media presence. For example, a product launch could be supported by high-quality photos, a behind-the-scenes video, and an infographic detailing the product's features and benefits. This multifaceted approach caters to different audience preferences and keeps your content fresh and interesting.

To effectively leverage visual content, it's essential to use the right tools and resources. Photo editing tools like Adobe Lightroom and Snapseed, video editing software like Adobe Premiere Pro and Final Cut Pro, and graphic design platforms like Canva and Adobe Spark can help you create professional-quality visuals even without extensive design skills. Additionally, leveraging social media analytics can provide insights into which types of visual content resonate most with your audience, allowing you to refine your strategy and focus on what works best.

Photos, videos, and graphics are indispensable components of a successful social media marketing strategy. Each type of visual content offers unique benefits and can be used to convey your brand's message in a compelling and engaging way.

2.4 The Power of Storytelling in Social Media

Storytelling is a timeless and powerful tool in social media marketing, capable of transforming mundane content into engaging and memorable experiences. The power of storytelling lies in its ability to connect with audiences on an emotional level, making your brand more relatable and compelling. In the fast-paced world of social media, where users are bombarded with a constant stream of information, stories stand out as a way to capture attention and foster deeper connections.

Storytelling in social media involves crafting narratives that resonate with your audience's values, desires, and experiences. Instead of merely presenting facts or promoting products, effective storytelling weaves these elements into a cohesive and engaging narrative. This approach humanizes your brand, turning it into a character in a story that your audience cares about and follows.

One of the key elements of storytelling is authenticity. Audiences are drawn to genuine stories that reflect real experiences and emotions. Sharing behind-the-scenes content, personal anecdotes, and customer stories can create a sense of authenticity that builds trust and loyalty. For example, a brand can share the journey of how a product was developed, highlighting the challenges and triumphs along the way. This not only informs the audience but also creates an emotional connection, making them feel invested in the brand's success.

User-generated content (UGC) is another powerful aspect of storytelling. Encouraging your customers to share their experiences with your products or services allows them to become part of your brand's story. UGC not only provides authentic content but also fosters a sense of community and belonging among your audience. Featuring these stories on your social media channels can amplify their reach and impact, as people are more likely to trust and relate to content created by their peers.

Visual storytelling is particularly effective on social media, where visual content tends to perform better than text alone. Combining images, videos, and graphics with a compelling narrative can enhance the storytelling experience. Platforms like Instagram and Snapchat, with their Stories feature, allow brands to create immersive, short-lived narratives that keep audiences engaged. These stories can include a mix of photos, videos, text overlays, and interactive elements like polls and questions, providing a dynamic and interactive experience.

Consistency is crucial in storytelling. A consistent brand narrative helps reinforce your message and ensures that your audience recognizes and remembers your story. This involves maintaining a cohesive voice, tone, and visual style across all your social media channels. Whether you're sharing a customer testimonial, a behind-the-scenes look, or a product launch, the underlying story should align with your brand's core values and mission.

Emotional appeal is another vital component. Stories that evoke emotions such as joy, surprise, sadness, or inspiration are more likely to be shared and remembered. Emotional storytelling can create a lasting impact, driving engagement and loyalty. For instance, a brand might share stories of how their products have positively impacted customers' lives, evoking feelings of gratitude and connection.

Interactive storytelling can also enhance engagement. Using features like polls, quizzes, and live videos, brands can create interactive narratives that involve the audience in the storytelling process. This not only keeps the audience engaged but also makes them feel like active participants in the brand's story.

storytelling is a powerful tool in social media marketing that goes beyond traditional advertising to create meaningful and memorable connections with your audience.

2.5 Content Calendar and Scheduling

A well-organized content calendar and strategic scheduling are essential components of a successful social media marketing plan. They ensure that your content is consistently delivered to your audience, align with your marketing goals, and optimize your reach and engagement.

Creating a Content Calendar involves mapping out your content in advance, typically on a monthly or quarterly basis. This calendar should include the type of content you plan to post, the platform it will be shared on, the date and time of publication, and any relevant themes or campaigns. A content calendar helps you visualize your overall strategy, ensuring a balanced mix of content types and topics. It also allows you to plan around important dates, such as holidays, product launches, and promotional events, ensuring that your content remains timely and relevant.

Consistency is key in social media marketing, and a content calendar helps you maintain it. Regular posting keeps your audience engaged and increases the likelihood that your content will be seen. Depending on the platform and your audience's preferences, you might post several times a day on Twitter, daily on Instagram and Facebook, and a few times a week on LinkedIn. The content calendar helps you adhere to this schedule, ensuring that you never miss an opportunity to connect with your audience.

Scheduling Tools are invaluable for managing your content calendar. Platforms like Hootsuite, Buffer, and Sprout Social allow you to schedule posts in advance, saving you time and ensuring that your content is published at optimal times. These tools often come with analytics features, helping you determine the best times to post based on your audience's activity patterns.

Planning Content Themes is another benefit of a content calendar. For example, you might have "Motivation Mondays" where you share inspirational quotes, "Tutorial Tuesdays" for how-to guides, and "Feature Fridays" where you highlight customer stories or products. This thematic approach makes content creation easier and ensures a balanced mix of posts.

Aligning with Marketing Goals is crucial, and a content calendar helps you do this. Each piece of content should serve a specific purpose, whether it's driving traffic to your website, increasing brand awareness, or generating leads.

Flexibility is also important in content scheduling. While planning is essential, the social media landscape is dynamic, and unexpected events or trends can arise. Your content calendar should be flexible enough to accommodate real-time updates and adjustments. This might mean shifting scheduled posts to make room for timely content or quickly responding to breaking news relevant to your industry.

Monitoring and Adjusting your content calendar is an ongoing process. Regularly review your analytics to see which types of content are performing best and adjust your strategy accordingly. This might involve increasing the frequency of popular content types, experimenting with new formats, or refining your posting times. Continuous monitoring and tweaking ensure that your content strategy remains effective and responsive to your audience's needs.

A well-structured content calendar and strategic scheduling are essential for consistent, engaging, and effective social media marketing.

2.6 User-Generated Content and Community Building

User-generated content (UGC) is a powerful asset in social media marketing, playing a crucial role in community building and enhancing brand authenticity. UGC includes any content—such as photos, videos, reviews, and testimonials—created by your customers or followers, rather than by your brand. Leveraging UGC not only amplifies your marketing efforts but also fosters a sense of community and trust among your audience.

The Value of UGC lies in its authenticity. Consumers tend to trust content created by their peers more than branded content. When users see real people using and enjoying your products, it adds credibility and can significantly influence their purchasing decisions. UGC serves as social proof, demonstrating that your brand delivers on its promises and that your customers are genuinely satisfied.

Encouraging UGC involves creating opportunities and incentives for your audience to share their experiences. This can be done through contests, hashtags, challenges, and calls-to-action. For example, you might run a photo contest where customers share pictures of themselves using your product with a specific hashtag, offering a prize for the best submission. This not only generates valuable content but also increases engagement and reach as users share their posts with their own networks.

Showcasing UGC on your social media platforms is essential for building a sense of community. This can be done through reposting user photos, sharing customer testimonials, or creating highlight reels of user content. Tagging and mentioning the original creators in your posts further strengthens the bond and encourages more users to contribute.

Building a Community around UGC involves active engagement and interaction. Respond to user posts, comments, and messages to show that you are listening and appreciate their contributions. Host interactive events like live Q&A sessions, webinars, and virtual meetups to foster real-time connections and discussions. Creating a community space, such as a Facebook group or a branded hashtag on Instagram, provides a dedicated platform for your audience to share their experiences, ask questions, and connect with like-minded individuals.

Leveraging Influencers and Advocates can amplify your UGC efforts. Collaborate with influencers who align with your brand values and have a strong, engaged following. Influencers can generate high-quality UGC and encourage their followers to do the same, expanding your reach and credibility. Identify and nurture brand advocates—loyal customers who are passionate about your brand and naturally share their positive experiences. Recognize and reward these advocates to strengthen their connection to your brand and motivate others to follow suit.

Measuring the Impact of UGC on your community-building efforts is crucial for refining your strategy. Track metrics such as engagement rates, the volume of UGC created, hashtag usage, and the growth of your online community. Analyzing these metrics helps you understand the effectiveness of your UGC initiatives and identify areas for improvement. Additionally, gather qualitative feedback from your community to gain insights into their experiences and preferences.

Maintaining a Safe and Positive Environment is essential for sustaining a vibrant community. Establish clear guidelines for behavior and content to ensure that your community remains welcoming and inclusive. Monitor your platforms for inappropriate content and address any issues promptly.

user-generated content is a vital component of social media marketing, driving community building and enhancing brand authenticity. Encouraging and showcasing UGC, actively engaging with your audience, leveraging influencers and advocates, measuring impact, and maintaining a positive environment, you can create a thriving community that supports and amplifies your brand. This community-centric approach not only boosts engagement and trust but also cultivates loyal customers who are passionate about your brand and eager to share their experiences.

2.7 Collaborating with Influencers and Brand Ambassadors

Collaborating with influencers and brand ambassadors is a highly effective strategy in social media marketing, offering the potential to extend your reach, enhance credibility, and foster deeper connections with your target audience. Influencers and brand ambassadors, with their established followings and trusted voices, can help amplify your brand message and drive engagement in a way that traditional advertising often cannot.

Understanding the Role of Influencers involves recognizing their ability to sway the opinions and behaviors of their followers. Influencers come in various tiers, from mega-influencers with millions of followers to micro-influencers who have smaller, but highly engaged, audiences. Each type of influencer offers unique advantages. Mega-influencers provide vast reach and visibility, while micro-influencers often have more authentic and personal connections with their followers, leading to higher engagement rates. Selecting the right type of influencer depends on your campaign goals, target audience, and budget.

Identifying the Right Influencers for your brand is crucial. Look for influencers whose values, aesthetics, and audience align with your brand. Authenticity is key, so prioritize influencers who have a genuine connection to your industry or product. Tools like BuzzSumo, Social Blade, and influencer marketing platforms can help you find and evaluate potential influencers based on their reach, engagement, and relevance to your brand. Additionally, consider factors such as the influencer's content style, past collaborations, and audience demographics.

Establishing Clear Objectives and Expectations is essential for a successful collaboration. Define the goals of your influencer campaign, whether it's increasing brand awareness, driving sales, or generating user-generated content. Communicate these objectives clearly to your influencers, along with specific deliverables, timelines, and key messages. Providing creative freedom within these guidelines allows influencers to craft content that resonates authentically with their audience while aligning with your brand goals.

Building Long-Term Relationships with Brand Ambassadors can be more beneficial than one-off collaborations. Brand ambassadors are loyal advocates who consistently promote your brand over an extended period. These partnerships foster deeper trust and loyalty among their followers. Identify and nurture potential brand ambassadors from your existing customer base, employees, or micro-influencers who genuinely love your brand. Offer them exclusive perks, early access to products, and opportunities for deeper engagement with your brand to strengthen their commitment.

Collaborative Content Creation allows for a more integrated and authentic partnership. Work with influencers and brand ambassadors to co-create content that highlights your brand's unique value proposition. This could include product reviews, tutorials, behind-the-scenes looks, and lifestyle content. The key is to ensure the content feels natural and engaging, leveraging the influencer's unique voice and style. Collaborative content not only drives engagement but also fosters a sense of authenticity and trust.

Measuring the Success of Influencer Collaborations is crucial to understanding their impact and refining your strategy. Track metrics such as engagement rates, follower growth, website traffic, and sales conversions to gauge the effectiveness of your influencer campaigns. Use UTM parameters and unique discount codes to measure the direct impact of influencer-driven traffic and sales. Additionally, qualitative feedback from the influencer and their audience can provide valuable insights into the campaign's success and areas for improvement.

Navigating Legal and Ethical Considerations is an important aspect of influencer marketing. Ensure that all collaborations comply with advertising regulations and platform-specific guidelines. Influencers should clearly disclose sponsored content to maintain transparency and trust with their audience. Providing clear contracts and agreements outlining expectations, compensation, and disclosure requirements helps protect both parties and ensures a smooth collaboration.

Leveraging Influencer Insights and Feedback can enhance your overall marketing strategy. Influencers often have deep insights into their audience's preferences and trends. Engaging in open dialogue with them can provide valuable feedback on your products, marketing messages, and campaign effectiveness. Use this feedback to refine your strategies, improve your offerings, and stay ahead of market trends.

collaborating with influencers and brand ambassadors can significantly amplify your social media marketing efforts. Carefully selecting the right partners, establishing clear objectives, fostering long-term relationships, co-creating engaging content, measuring success, and adhering to legal and ethical standards, you can leverage their influence to build trust, drive engagement, and achieve your marketing goals. This strategic approach not only enhances your brand's visibility and credibility but also creates a dynamic and authentic connection with your audience.

2.8 Writing Effective Captions and Call-to-Actions

Crafting effective captions and calls-to-action (CTAs) is crucial for driving engagement and achieving your marketing objectives on social media. Captions provide context to your visual content, making it more relatable and compelling, while CTAs guide your audience towards taking desired actions, such as liking, commenting, sharing, or visiting your website.

The Art of Writing Captions involves blending creativity, clarity, and relevance. An engaging caption should capture attention, convey your message succinctly, and resonate with your audience. Start by grabbing attention with a strong opening line. This could be a provocative question, a surprising fact, or a compelling statement that piques curiosity. For example, a travel brand might begin with, "Ever dreamt of waking up to the sound of ocean waves?" This immediately draws the reader in and sets the stage for the rest of the caption.

Keeping Captions Concise and Relevant is key to maintaining your audience's interest. Social media users typically scroll quickly through their feeds, so long-winded captions might be overlooked. Aim to convey your message in a clear and concise manner. Use short sentences and paragraphs to make your captions easily digestible. At the same time, ensure that your captions are relevant to the visual content they accompany. This coherence reinforces your message and makes the overall post more impactful.

Injecting Personality and Emotion into your captions can make them more relatable and engaging. Whether your brand's tone is humorous, inspirational, or informative, let it shine through in your writing. Use emojis, colloquial language, and personal anecdotes to add a human touch. For instance, a fitness brand might write, "Feeling the burn never felt so good! 🔥 What's your post-workout treat?" This type of caption not only reflects the brand's personality but also encourages interaction.

Utilizing Hashtags Strategically can expand your reach and visibility. Hashtags categorize your content and make it discoverable to users interested in specific topics. Research and use relevant hashtags that align with your post and target audience. While it's beneficial to include popular hashtags, don't overlook niche or branded hashtags that can connect you with a more targeted audience. For example, a beauty brand might use #MakeupMonday alongside #EcoFriendlyBeauty to tap into both broad and specific conversations.

Crafting Effective CTAs is essential for driving engagement and achieving your social media goals. A CTA directs your audience towards taking a specific action, such as visiting your website, signing up for a newsletter, or participating in a contest. To be effective, a CTA should be clear, concise, and compelling. Use action-oriented language that creates a sense of urgency or excitement. For example, "Swipe up to discover our summer collection!" or "Tag a friend who needs to see this!" These prompts encourage immediate action and can significantly boost engagement.

Aligning CTAs with Marketing Objectives ensures that each post contributes to your broader goals. If your objective is to increase website traffic, your CTA might encourage users to click a link in your bio or swipe up in a Story. If your goal is to boost engagement, you might ask followers to comment on their opinions or share your post with friends. Tailoring your CTAs to your specific objectives helps maximize the impact of your social media efforts.

Testing and Optimizing Captions and CTAs is an ongoing process.

Experiment with different styles, lengths, and tones to see what resonates best with your audience. Analyze the performance of your posts using social media analytics tools, looking at metrics such as engagement rates, click-through rates, and conversion rates. Use this data to refine your approach, focusing on the types of captions and CTAs that drive the most engagement and desired actions.

Writing effective captions and CTAs is a skill that can significantly enhance your social media marketing efforts. Creating engaging, concise, and relevant captions, injecting personality and emotion, utilizing hashtags strategically, crafting compelling CTAs, aligning them with your marketing objectives, and continually testing and optimizing, you can capture your audience's attention, encourage interaction, and drive meaningful actions that support your overall marketing strategy.

2.8 Writing Effective Captions and Call-to-Actions

Writing effective captions and calls-to-action (CTAs) is an essential skill in social media marketing. Captions add context, personality, and engagement to your posts, while CTAs drive your audience to take specific actions that align with your marketing goals. Mastering the art of crafting these elements can significantly enhance your social media presence and boost engagement.

Creating Compelling Captions involves a blend of creativity, clarity, and relevance. An effective caption should capture attention, provide context, and invite interaction. Start with a strong opening line to grab your audience's attention. This could be a question, a bold statement, or an intriguing fact. For instance, a fashion brand might start a caption with, "Ready to elevate your style game?" This immediately draws the reader in and sets the tone for the rest of the caption.

Keep It Concise and Clear: Social media users often scroll quickly through their feeds, so your caption needs to be clear and to the point. Avoid overly long or complex sentences. Instead, aim for brevity while still conveying your message effectively. Use short paragraphs or bullet points to break up the text and make it more digestible.

Add Personality and Emotion: Your captions should reflect your brand's voice and personality. Whether your tone is playful, professional, or inspirational, make sure it shines through in your writing. Using emojis, humor, or storytelling can add a personal touch and make your content more relatable. For example, a food brand might write, "Nothing beats the smell of fresh-baked cookies ☐ What's your favorite homemade treat?"

Incorporate Relevant Hashtags: Hashtags are a powerful tool for increasing the discoverability of your posts. Use a mix of popular and niche hashtags relevant to your content and audience. While popular hashtags can broaden your reach, niche hashtags can connect you with a more targeted audience. For instance, a travel brand might use #TravelTuesday for a general audience and #HiddenGemsItaly for a specific post about lesser-known Italian destinations.

Crafting Effective CTAs: Calls-to-action are essential for guiding your audience towards taking specific actions. An effective CTA should be clear, direct, and compelling. Use action-oriented language to create a sense of urgency or excitement. For example, "Shop now and get 20% off!" or "Share your thoughts in the comments below!"

Align CTAs with Your Goals: Ensure that your CTAs are aligned with your overall marketing objectives. If your goal is to increase engagement, you might ask followers to comment or share your post. If you want to drive traffic to your website, encourage them to click the link in your bio. Tailoring your CTAs to your goals helps maximize their effectiveness.

Test and Optimize: Regularly test different types of captions and CTAs to see what resonates best with your audience. Use A/B testing to compare variations and analyze which performs better. Pay attention to metrics like engagement rates, click-through rates, and conversion rates. Use these insights to refine your approach and continually improve your content.

Use Analytics to Guide Your Strategy: Utilize social media analytics tools to track the performance of your captions and CTAs. Analyze data such as likes, shares, comments, and clicks to understand what works and what doesn't. This data-driven approach allows you to make informed decisions and optimize your strategy for better results.

Be Authentic and Transparent: Authenticity is crucial in social media marketing. Ensure that your captions and CTAs reflect genuine intentions and avoid being overly promotional. Transparency builds trust with your audience and fosters long-term loyalty.

Encourage User Interaction: Inviting your audience to engage with your content can significantly boost interaction. Ask questions, encourage comments, and prompt users to share their experiences. For example, a fitness brand might ask, "What's your favorite way to stay active on weekends? Let us know in the comments!"

writing effective captions and CTAs is a key component of successful social media marketing.

2.9 Leveraging Hashtags for Greater Reach

Hashtags are a powerful tool in social media marketing, offering a way to increase the discoverability of your content, engage with a wider audience, and participate in relevant conversations. When used strategically, hashtags can significantly boost your reach and enhance the visibility of your brand. Here's how you can effectively leverage hashtags for greater reach on social media.

Understanding Hashtags: At their core, hashtags are keywords or phrases preceded by the pound sign (#) that categorize content and make it searchable. When users click on or search for a specific hashtag, they can see all the posts that include it. This functionality allows your content to be discovered by users who are interested in that particular topic, even if they don't follow your account.

Researching Relevant Hashtags: The first step in leveraging hashtags is to identify the ones that are relevant to your brand, industry, and audience. Start by researching what hashtags your competitors and industry leaders are using. Tools like Hashtagify, RiteTag, and the built-in search features on platforms like Instagram and Twitter can help you find popular and trending hashtags. Aim to use a mix of broad, widely-used hashtags and more specific, niche ones to reach different segments of your audience.

Using a Mix of Hashtag Types: Different types of hashtags serve different purposes. Broad hashtags like #travel, #food, or #fashion have a vast reach but also a lot of competition. Niche hashtags, such as #EcoFriendlyTravel or #VeganRecipes, target a more specific audience and can lead to higher engagement. Branded hashtags, which are unique to your business or campaign, help build brand identity and encourage user-generated content. Event-specific hashtags, like #SuperBowl or #BlackFriday, can tap into large-scale conversations and increase visibility during peak times.

Optimal Number of Hashtags: The optimal number of hashtags varies by platform. On Instagram, using up to 30 hashtags can be effective, but studies suggest that engagement peaks with around 9 to 11 hashtags per post. On Twitter, where brevity is key, using 1 to 2 hashtags per tweet is recommended. Facebook posts benefit from using fewer hashtags, typically 1 to 3, while LinkedIn suggests using 3 to 5 hashtags per post. Experiment with different quantities to find what works best for your audience and platform.

Creating Branded Hashtags: Branded hashtags are unique to your business and can be used to promote your brand, campaigns, or events. They are an excellent way to encourage user-generated content and build community. For example, a fitness brand might create a hashtag like #FitWithUs to motivate customers to share their workout photos. Encourage your followers to use your branded hashtags by featuring their posts on your profile, offering incentives, or running contests.

Engaging with Hashtag Communities: Participating in hashtag communities helps you connect with users who share similar interests. Engage with posts that use the same hashtags by liking, commenting, and sharing content. This interaction not only increases your visibility but also fosters relationships with potential customers and influencers in your industry.

Monitoring Hashtag Performance: Regularly analyze the performance of the hashtags you use to understand which ones drive the most engagement and reach. Social media analytics tools can provide insights into how different hashtags perform in terms of likes, shares, comments, and impressions. Use this data to refine your hashtag strategy, focusing on the ones that yield the best results.

Avoiding Hashtag Mistakes: Overusing hashtags, using irrelevant or overly generic hashtags, and failing to research the meaning or popularity of a hashtag can negatively impact your reach and brand image. Ensure that the hashtags you use are relevant to your content and resonate with your target audience. Avoid banned or spammy hashtags that can reduce your visibility or result in your content being flagged.

Adapting to Platform-Specific Trends: Hashtag trends can vary significantly between platforms. Stay updated on the latest trends and popular hashtags on each social media platform you use. For instance, TikTok often has trending challenges and hashtags that can give your content a significant boost if you participate early. Similarly, Instagram's Explore page can highlight trending hashtags and topics relevant to your niche.

Leveraging hashtags effectively requires a strategic approach tailored to your brand and audience. Researching relevant hashtags, using a mix of broad and niche tags, creating branded hashtags, engaging with hashtag communities, monitoring performance, and adapting to platform-specific trends, you can maximize your reach and visibility on social media, ultimately driving greater engagement and success for your brand.

2.10 Tools and Resources for Content Creation

In the fast-paced world of social media marketing, having the right tools and resources for content creation can significantly streamline your workflow and enhance the quality of your output. These tools can help you create visually appealing graphics, engaging videos, well-written posts, and more. Here are some of the most useful tools and resources that can elevate your social media content creation.

1. Graphic Design Tools:

- Canva: Canva is a user-friendly graphic design tool that offers a wide range of templates for social media posts, infographics, presentations, and more. Its drag-and-drop interface and extensive library of images, fonts, and icons make it easy to create professional-quality designs even if you have no prior design experience.

- Adobe Spark: Adobe Spark is another versatile design tool that allows you to create stunning graphics, videos, and web pages. It's perfect for quick and impactful social media content and integrates well with other Adobe products.

- Piktochart: Piktochart is an excellent tool for creating infographics and data visualizations. It offers customizable templates and an intuitive interface, making it easy to turn complex information into visually appealing graphics.

2. Video Creation and Editing Tools:

- Adobe Premiere Pro: Adobe Premiere Pro is a professional video editing software that provides comprehensive tools for editing and producing high-quality videos. It's widely used in the industry for its robust features and versatility.

- iMovie: For Mac users, iMovie offers a simpler, more

accessible video editing option. It's great for creating polished videos with basic editing needs.

- Animoto: Animoto is a cloud-based video creation tool that allows you to create videos using templates. It's particularly useful for creating quick promotional videos, social media ads, and video slideshows.

3. Content Planning and Scheduling Tools:

- Hootsuite: Hootsuite is a comprehensive social media management platform that allows you to schedule posts, monitor social media activity, and analyze performance across multiple social media platforms. Its content calendar feature helps you plan and organize your content efficiently.

- Buffer: Buffer is another popular social media scheduling tool that simplifies the process of planning, scheduling, and publishing content. It also provides analytics to help you measure the performance of your posts.

- CoSchedule: CoSchedule offers a marketing calendar and suite of tools for scheduling, organizing, and executing your content marketing strategy. It integrates well with WordPress, social media platforms, and other marketing tools.

4. Photo Editing Tools:

- Adobe Lightroom: Adobe Lightroom is a powerful photo editing tool that offers advanced features for enhancing and editing photos. It's ideal for creating consistent, high-quality visuals for your social media profiles.

- Snapseed: Snapseed is a mobile photo editing app by Google that offers a range of professional-grade editing tools. It's user-friendly and great for on-the-go photo enhancements.

- VSCO: VSCO is both a photo editing app and a social network. It provides a variety of filters and editing tools to give your photos a unique look, perfect for maintaining a consistent aesthetic on platforms like Instagram.

5. Writing and Copyediting Tools:

- Grammarly: Grammarly is a writing assistant that helps you improve your writing by checking for grammar, punctuation, and style errors. It's essential for ensuring that your social media posts are clear, professional, and error-free.

- Hemingway Editor: The Hemingway Editor helps you write more concisely and clearly by highlighting complex sentences and common errors. It's a great tool for refining your social media copy.

- CoSchedule Headline Analyzer: This tool helps you craft compelling headlines by analyzing their effectiveness based on various factors. It's particularly useful for creating attention-grabbing titles for your blog posts and social media updates.

6. Stock Photos and Videos:

- Unsplash: Unsplash offers a vast library of high-quality, royalty-free photos that you can use for your social media posts. The photos are contributed by a global community of photographers and are free to use.

- Pexels: Pexels provides free stock photos and videos that are perfect for enhancing your social media content. The site's extensive collection makes it easy to find visuals that match your brand's aesthetic.

- Shutterstock: For those willing to invest in premium stock photos and videos, Shutterstock offers a wide variety of high-quality assets. It's a go-to resource for professional-grade visuals.

7. Interactive Content Tools:

- Typeform: Typeform allows you to create engaging surveys, quizzes, and forms. Its interactive format can help you gather valuable feedback from your audience and increase engagement.

- Poll Everywhere: Poll Everywhere is a tool for creating live polls and interactive questions. It's great for engaging your audience during live events or webinars.

8. Analytics and Performance Tools:

- Google Analytics: Google Analytics provides in-depth insights into your website traffic and social media performance. It's essential for understanding how your audience interacts with your content and identifying areas for improvement.

- Socialbakers: Socialbakers offers a suite of tools for analyzing and optimizing your social media performance. It provides comprehensive analytics, benchmarking, and audience insights.

Leveraging these tools and resources, you can streamline your content creation process, enhance the quality of your social media posts, and ultimately achieve greater success in your social media marketing efforts. Whether you're creating graphics, editing videos, scheduling posts, or analyzing performance, these tools provide the functionality and efficiency needed to excel in the dynamic world of social media.

CHAPTER 3: MARKETING STRATEGIES

F acebook remains one of the most powerful platforms for social media marketing, offering businesses a diverse array of tools and features to connect with their audience and drive engagement. Effective Facebook marketing begins with creating a well-optimized business page that accurately reflects your brand's identity, complete with a compelling profile picture, cover photo, and a detailed "About" section. Consistency in posting is crucial; sharing a mix of content types, such as images, videos, articles, and infographics, can keep your audience engaged. Utilizing Facebook's robust targeting options allows you to reach specific demographics, interests, and behaviors, making your ads more relevant and effective. Engaging with your audience through comments, messages, and interactive posts like polls and questions helps build a community around your brand. Facebook Live is another powerful tool for real-time engagement, allowing you to host live events, Q&A sessions, and product launches. Additionally, leveraging Facebook Groups can foster a more intimate and active community, providing a space for loyal followers to interact and share experiences. Analyzing performance metrics with Facebook Insights is essential to understand what content resonates most with your audience and to refine your strategy accordingly.

3.2 Instagram Marketing Strategies

Instagram is a visually-driven platform that offers a plethora of opportunities for brands to showcase their products and services in creative and engaging ways. To effectively leverage Instagram for marketing, start by crafting a visually cohesive and appealing profile that aligns with your brand's identity. Use high-quality images, compelling captions, and a consistent color palette to create a recognizable aesthetic. Instagram Stories, with their ephemeral nature, are perfect for sharing behind-the-scenes content, special promotions, and interactive elements like polls and questions that engage your audience in real-time.

Utilizing Instagram's various features, such as IGTV for long-form video content and Reels for short, engaging clips, can help diversify your content and reach different segments of your audience. Hashtags play a crucial role on Instagram; using a mix of popular, niche, and branded hashtags can increase your content's discoverability and attract a broader audience. Influencer collaborations are particularly effective on Instagram, where visually appealing and authentic content resonates strongly. Partnering with influencers who align with your brand can amplify your reach and lend credibility through their trusted voices.

Regularly engaging with your audience through comments, likes, and direct messages fosters a sense of community and loyalty. Running Instagram contests or giveaways can also boost engagement and attract new followers. Instagram Shopping and Shoppable posts make it easy for users to purchase products directly from the app, streamlining the shopping experience and driving conversions. Finally, analyzing insights provided by Instagram can help you understand your audience's behavior, identify top-performing content, and refine your strategy to improve engagement and growth.

3.3 Twitter Marketing Strategies

Twitter is a fast-paced platform known for its real-time updates and concise communication, making it a powerful tool for brands to engage with their audience, participate in trending conversations, and amplify their message. To effectively market on Twitter, it is crucial to maintain a consistent posting schedule with a mix of promotional content, industry news, and engaging tweets that reflect your brand's personality. Utilizing Twitter's character limit to craft sharp, witty, and informative messages can help capture attention and drive engagement.

Hashtags are vital on Twitter, as they help categorize content and increase visibility in relevant conversations. Using trending and relevant hashtags strategically can boost the reach of your tweets and connect you with a broader audience. Additionally, creating branded hashtags for campaigns or events can foster community and brand recognition.

Engaging directly with your audience is a cornerstone of successful Twitter marketing. Responding to mentions, retweeting user-generated content, and participating in discussions show that your brand is approachable and attentive. Twitter Chats, which are organized around specific hashtags, can position your brand as a thought leader and create opportunities for direct interaction with your followers.

Promoted Tweets and Twitter Ads offer targeted advertising options to increase your visibility and reach specific demographics based on interests, behaviors, and geographic locations. These paid options can effectively boost the impact of key messages or campaigns.

Visual content, including images, GIFs, and videos, can enhance your tweets and make them more engaging. Twitter polls are another interactive feature that can increase engagement and gather valuable insights from your audience.

Monitoring and analyzing performance metrics through Twitter Analytics allows you to track the effectiveness of your strategies.

Key metrics such as engagement rates, retweets, and mentions provide insights into what content resonates with your audience and how to optimize future tweets.

Implementing these strategies, brands can harness Twitter's unique capabilities to connect with their audience in real-time, drive engagement, and build a dynamic online presence.

3.4 LinkedIn Marketing Strategies

LinkedIn is the premier social media platform for professionals and businesses, making it an essential tool for B2B marketing, networking, and establishing thought leadership. To effectively market on LinkedIn, start by creating a comprehensive and professional company page that showcases your brand's mission, values, and services. A well-optimized profile with a high-quality logo, compelling banner image, and detailed description can enhance your brand's credibility and attract followers.

Content is king on LinkedIn, and sharing high-quality, relevant content regularly can position your brand as an industry leader. This includes a mix of articles, industry news, thought leadership pieces, and company updates. Long-form content, such as blog posts and whitepapers, can drive engagement and encourage sharing. Additionally, LinkedIn Pulse offers a platform for publishing articles directly on LinkedIn, expanding your reach and establishing your authority on key topics.

Engaging with your audience on LinkedIn is crucial. Respond to comments on your posts, participate in relevant discussions, and join industry-specific groups to connect with potential clients and partners. LinkedIn Groups provide a valuable opportunity to share expertise, engage in discussions, and network with professionals in your field. Creating your own group around a specific niche or interest can further establish your brand as a leader and foster a community around your business.

LinkedIn's targeted advertising options, such as Sponsored Content, Sponsored InMail, and Text Ads, allow you to reach specific professional demographics, including job titles, industries, and company sizes. These tools can be highly effective for lead generation, promoting events, and driving traffic to your website.

Showcasing your company culture and employee achievements can humanize your brand and attract top talent. Share behind-the-scenes looks, employee stories, and company milestones to give a personal touch to your professional image. LinkedIn's recommendation feature allows satisfied clients and partners to endorse your services, adding another layer of credibility to your profile.

Leveraging LinkedIn Analytics is crucial for measuring the success of your marketing efforts. Track metrics such as engagement rates, follower growth, and post performance to gain insights into what resonates with your audience and refine your strategy accordingly.

3.5 Pinterest Marketing Strategies

Pinterest is a visual discovery and bookmarking platform that offers unique opportunities for brands to showcase their products and ideas in an engaging and visually appealing manner. To effectively market on Pinterest, start by creating a business account and optimizing your profile with a clear and compelling description, a high-quality profile picture, and a link to your website. A well-crafted profile sets the stage for attracting followers and driving traffic to your site.

Creating and Organizing Boards is fundamental to Pinterest marketing. Boards should be organized around specific themes, interests, or categories that align with your brand and audience's interests. For instance, a home decor brand might create boards for different styles, such as "Modern Living Rooms" or "Rustic Kitchen Ideas." Each board should have a descriptive title and an engaging cover image to attract users' attention.

Pinning High-Quality Content is crucial for success on Pinterest.

Pins should be visually appealing, with high-resolution images and clear, concise descriptions. Vertical images perform best on Pinterest due to the platform's layout, and using rich pins—pins that include additional information like product details or recipes —can enhance the user experience and increase engagement. Consistently pinning fresh content and repinning popular pins from other users can keep your boards active and engaging.

Leveraging Keywords in your pin descriptions and board titles is essential for improving discoverability. Pinterest operates as a search engine, so incorporating relevant keywords can help your content appear in search results. Research trending keywords and phrases related to your industry and integrate them naturally into your descriptions to attract a broader audience.

Using Pinterest Analytics is vital for understanding what types of content resonate with your audience. Pinterest Analytics provides insights into your most popular pins, boards, and audience demographics. Use this data to refine your strategy, focusing on the content that drives the most engagement and traffic. Tracking metrics such as repins, clicks, and impressions can help you identify successful trends and optimize your future content.

Engaging with Your Community by following relevant accounts, repinning user content, and responding to comments can foster a sense of community and increase your visibility. Collaborative boards, where multiple users contribute pins, can also expand your reach and expose your brand to new audiences.

Promoted Pins offer targeted advertising options to reach specific demographics and interests. Promoted Pins blend seamlessly with organic content, making them less intrusive and more likely to engage users. Setting clear objectives for your promoted pin campaigns, such as increasing website traffic or boosting brand awareness, can help you measure their effectiveness and adjust your strategy accordingly.

Seasonal and Trend-Based Content can significantly boost your engagement on Pinterest. Plan your content calendar around holidays, seasonal trends, and events relevant to your audience. For example, a fashion brand might create a board for "Spring Fashion Trends" or "Holiday Party Outfits." Staying current with trends and tailoring your content to seasonal interests can drive higher engagement and keep your boards relevant.

Utilizing Pinterest's Visual Search Tool can enhance your content's discoverability. The visual search tool allows users to find pins similar to an image they are interested in.

Pinterest offers a unique platform for visually driven marketing, allowing brands to showcase their products and ideas in an engaging way. Creating organized and themed boards, pinning high-quality content, leveraging keywords, using analytics, engaging with the community, utilizing promoted pins, focusing on seasonal trends, and optimizing for visual search, you can effectively use Pinterest to increase brand visibility, drive traffic, and engage with a broader audience.

3.6 YouTube Marketing Strategies

YouTube is the largest video-sharing platform globally, providing businesses with a powerful medium to reach and engage with a vast audience. To effectively market on YouTube, start by creating a branded channel that reflects your company's identity. This includes using a professional logo, a cohesive channel banner, and a detailed "About" section that clearly communicates what viewers can expect from your content.

Creating High-Quality Video Content is the cornerstone of a successful YouTube strategy. Focus on producing videos that provide value to your audience, whether through education, entertainment, or inspiration. Tutorials, product reviews, behind-the-scenes looks, customer testimonials, and industry insights are all effective content types. Ensure that your videos are well-scripted, visually appealing, and professionally edited to maintain a high production quality.

Optimizing Video Titles, Descriptions, and Tags is crucial for increasing discoverability. Use relevant keywords in your video titles and descriptions to improve search engine ranking and make it easier for users to find your content. Include a compelling and concise summary of the video in the description, along with links to your website, social media profiles, and related videos. Tags should be specific and relevant, helping YouTube's algorithm understand the content of your video and suggest it to the right audience.

Engaging Thumbnails and End Screens can significantly boost your video's click-through rate and viewer retention. Thumbnails should be visually compelling and accurately represent the content of the video. Custom thumbnails with text overlays can highlight key points and attract more clicks. End screens and cards are effective tools for encouraging viewers to take further actions, such as subscribing to your channel, watching another video, or visiting your website.

Consistency in Posting is vital to maintaining and growing your audience on YouTube. Develop a content calendar to plan and schedule your videos regularly. Consistent posting not only keeps your audience engaged but also signals to YouTube's algorithm that your channel is active, which can improve your visibility.

Engaging with Your Audience through comments, likes, and shares fosters a sense of community and loyalty. Respond to comments on your videos, ask for viewer feedback, and encourage discussions. Hosting live streams and Q&A sessions can provide real-time interaction and deepen your connection with your audience.

Collaborating with Influencers and Other Brands can expand your reach and introduce your channel to new audiences. Partner with influencers who have a substantial following in your industry, and consider guest appearances or co-hosted videos. These collaborations can enhance your credibility and attract more subscribers.

Utilizing YouTube Ads offers targeted advertising options to reach specific demographics and interests. Skippable and non-skippable video ads, bumper ads, and sponsored cards are various formats you can use to promote your content. Define clear goals for your ad campaigns, such as increasing brand awareness, driving traffic, or boosting sales, and measure their performance to optimize your strategy.

Analyzing Performance Metrics is essential for refining your YouTube strategy. Use YouTube Analytics to track key metrics such as views, watch time, audience retention, engagement, and subscriber growth. Analyzing this data helps you understand what content resonates with your audience and how you can improve future videos.

SEO and Cross-Promotion play a significant role in driving traffic to your YouTube channel. Optimize your channel and videos for search engines by using relevant keywords, metadata, and engaging content. Cross-promote your videos on your website, social media platforms, and email newsletters to increase visibility and attract a broader audience.

Creating Playlists and Series can enhance the user experience on your channel. Grouping related videos into playlists encourages viewers to watch multiple videos in a single session, increasing your overall watch time and improving your channel's performance. Series-based content, where videos build on each other, can keep viewers coming back for more.

YouTube offers a dynamic platform for video marketing, allowing brands to engage with a vast and diverse audience.

3.7 TikTok Marketing Strategies

TikTok, with its rapidly growing user base and highly engaging short-form video content, presents a unique opportunity for brands to reach younger, tech-savvy audiences. To effectively market on TikTok, it is essential to understand the platform's unique culture and leverage its features to create captivating content that resonates with users.

Understanding TikTok's Algorithm and Trends is crucial for success. TikTok's algorithm prioritizes content based on user interactions, video information, and device/account settings. Staying updated on trending sounds, challenges, and hashtags can help your content gain visibility. Engaging with trends early and creatively can increase your chances of appearing on the For You Page (FYP), where users discover new content.

Creating Authentic and Entertaining Content is key to engaging TikTok's audience. The platform thrives on creativity and authenticity, so polished, overly produced content may not perform as well. Focus on creating fun, relatable, and shareable videos that align with your brand's personality. Whether it's participating in viral challenges, showcasing behind-the-scenes moments, or creating how-to videos, ensure your content feels genuine and engaging.

Leveraging Hashtags and Challenges can amplify your reach. Hashtags categorize content and make it discoverable to users interested in specific topics. Using popular and relevant hashtags can increase your visibility. Additionally, creating branded hashtags and launching challenges can encourage user-generated content and increase engagement. For instance, a fitness brand might launch a challenge with a unique hashtag, encouraging users to share their workout routines.

Utilizing TikTok's Features such as Duets and Stitch can foster interaction and community engagement. Duets allow users to create videos alongside existing content, making it ideal for reactions, collaborations, and challenges. Stitch lets users incorporate segments of other TikTok videos into their own, promoting creativity and engagement. Encourage your audience to duet or stitch your content to increase interaction and reach.

Partnering with Influencers can significantly boost your brand's visibility and credibility. Influencers on TikTok have dedicated followings and can effectively promote your brand to their audience. Collaborate with influencers who align with your brand values and have a strong connection with your target demographic. Authentic influencer partnerships can drive higher engagement and conversions.

Running TikTok Ads provides targeted advertising options to reach specific demographics. TikTok offers various ad formats, including In-Feed Ads, Branded Hashtag Challenges, Branded Effects, and TopView Ads. Each format serves different purposes, from increasing brand awareness to driving traffic and conversions. Define your advertising goals and use TikTok's robust targeting options to reach the right audience.

Engaging with Your Audience through comments, likes, and shares is vital for building a community. Respond to comments on your videos, engage with user-generated content, and create content that encourages interaction. TikTok's community values authenticity and engagement, so active participation can enhance your brand's presence.

Using Analytics to Refine Your Strategy is essential for ongoing success. TikTok Pro Account offers analytics that provide insights into your content's performance, including views, likes, shares, and follower demographics. Analyzing these metrics helps you understand what types of content resonate with your audience and allows you to refine your strategy accordingly. Pay attention to trends in engagement and adjust your content plan to maximize impact.

Optimizing Posting Times can improve the visibility and engagement of your content. While there is no universal best time to post on TikTok, analyzing your audience's activity patterns can help you identify optimal posting times. Consistently posting when your audience is most active can increase the likelihood of your content being seen and engaged with.

Cross-Promoting Your TikTok Content on other social media platforms can drive traffic and increase your following. Share your TikTok videos on Instagram, Facebook, Twitter, and other channels to reach a broader audience. Include a call-to-action encouraging your followers on other platforms to follow you on TikTok.

TikTok offers a dynamic and engaging platform for brands to connect with a young, active audience.

3.8 Snapchat Marketing Strategies

Snapchat is a dynamic platform known for its ephemeral content and strong appeal to younger audiences. With features like Stories, Discover, and Snap Map, Snapchat offers unique opportunities for brands to connect with their audience in real-time and create engaging, short-lived content. To effectively market on Snapchat, it's important to understand the platform's nuances and leverage its features to create captivating and interactive content.

Creating Engaging Stories is at the heart of Snapchat marketing. Stories allow you to share a series of photos and videos that disappear after 24 hours, making them perfect for real-time updates, behind-the-scenes content, and daily engagement. Use Stories to showcase new products, share special promotions, highlight events, and provide a glimpse into your brand's culture. The ephemeral nature of Stories encourages users to check in regularly, fostering a sense of urgency and exclusivity.

Utilizing Filters and Lenses can enhance your content and make it more interactive. Snapchat's Geofilters and AR Lenses allow users to overlay fun and creative graphics on their photos and videos. Brands can create custom filters and lenses to promote events, campaigns, or new products. These tools not only make your content more engaging but also increase brand visibility as users share their snaps with your branded elements.

Leveraging Snap Ads offers targeted advertising options to reach specific demographics and interests. Snap Ads appear between user Stories and offer a seamless viewing experience. Formats include Snap Ads (vertical video ads), Collection Ads (allowing users to browse products), and Story Ads (a series of vertical ads within Discover). Use Snap Ads to drive traffic to your website, app downloads, or specific promotions. Snapchat's advanced targeting capabilities enable you to reach your ideal audience based on location, age, interests, and behaviors.

Exploring the Discover Feature allows brands to reach a wider audience through curated content. Discover features content from publishers, brands, and influencers. Collaborating with influencers or publishers who already have a strong presence on Discover can amplify your reach.

Utilizing Snap Map for Local Marketing is especially useful for businesses with physical locations. Snap Map allows users to share their location and see what's happening nearby. Hosting local events or offering special promotions can be highlighted on Snap Map to engage your community.

Running Contests and Giveaways can boost engagement and encourage user participation. Ask users to submit their snaps featuring your product or brand for a chance to win a prize. This not only generates user-generated content but also increases your brand's visibility as participants share their entries with their friends. Ensure the contest rules are clear and easy to follow, and promote the contest across all your social media channels.

Measuring Performance with Snapchat Analytics is crucial for understanding the effectiveness of your strategies. Snapchat Insights provides metrics such as story views, completion rates, and engagement rates. Analyze these metrics to see which types of content perform best and resonate with your audience. Use these insights to refine your content strategy, focusing on what drives the most engagement and conversions.

Engaging with Your Audience through direct interactions can build stronger connections. Respond to user snaps, participate in conversations, and show appreciation for your followers' content. Personalized interactions make your audience feel valued and more connected to your brand.

Cross-Promoting Snapchat Content on other social media

platforms can increase your reach and attract new followers. Share your Snapchat username and Snapcode on Instagram, Twitter, Facebook, and your website to encourage your audience to follow you on Snapchat. Highlight exclusive content or promotions available only on Snapchat to incentivize followers from other platforms to engage with your Snapchat content.

Snapchat offers a unique platform for creating engaging, ephemeral content that resonates with younger audiences.

3.9 Emerging Social Media Platforms

As the social media landscape continues to evolve, new platforms emerge, offering fresh opportunities for brands to engage with their audience and stay ahead of the competition. These emerging platforms often attract niche audiences and early adopters, making them ideal for innovative marketing strategies and targeting specific demographics. Here's a look at some of the emerging social media platforms that brands should consider incorporating into their marketing strategies.

Clubhouse is an audio-based social networking app that allows users to join or host live, interactive discussions on a variety of topics. This platform is ideal for brands looking to establish thought leadership, engage in real-time conversations, and build a community around their expertise. Hosting or participating in Clubhouse rooms can position your brand as a leader in your industry and provide a platform for authentic, in-depth discussions with your audience. To maximize your impact on Clubhouse, focus on creating valuable content, collaborating with influencers, and consistently engaging in relevant conversations.

Discord originally designed for gamers, has expanded to accommodate communities of all interests. It offers voice, video, and text communication channels, making it a versatile platform for building and nurturing communities. Brands can create their own servers on Discord to host discussions, share exclusive content, and provide customer support. The platform's emphasis on community and engagement makes it ideal for fostering strong relationships with your audience. To succeed on Discord, be active in your community, encourage user-generated content, and offer exclusive perks to members.

TikTok for Business while TikTok itself is not new, its business-specific tools and features continue to evolve, offering brands innovative ways to reach and engage with younger audiences. TikTok for Business provides a range of advertising options, including In-Feed Ads, Branded Hashtag Challenges, and Branded Effects. Brands can leverage TikTok's creative and viral nature to create compelling content that resonates with users. Focus on authenticity, creativity, and participation in trends to maximize your brand's visibility and engagement on TikTok.

Caffeine is a social broadcasting platform where users can host live shows and engage with viewers in real-time. This platform is particularly popular among gamers, musicians, and content creators. Brands can leverage Caffeine to host live events, product launches, and interactive sessions with their audience. The platform's real-time engagement features allow for immediate feedback and interaction, making it a powerful tool for building a loyal community. To succeed on Caffeine, focus on creating engaging live content and interacting directly with your viewers.

Vero positions itself as a more authentic and ad-free social media platform, emphasizing real connections and user control over their feed. Vero allows users to share photos, links, music, and more, categorizing their connections into close friends, friends, acquaintances, and followers. Brands can use Vero to connect with their audience on a more personal level, sharing content that aligns with their values and interests. Since Vero prioritizes organic reach over paid promotions, focus on creating high-quality, engaging content that encourages genuine interaction.

Houseparty is a group video chat app that integrates games and interactive features, making it a fun and engaging platform for social interaction. Brands can use Houseparty to host virtual events, game nights, and interactive sessions with their audience.

This platform is ideal for brands targeting a younger demographic and looking to create a playful, engaging presence. To make the most of Houseparty, create interactive and entertaining content that encourages participation and fosters a sense of community.

Triller is a social video platform similar to TikTok, where users can create and share short music videos and other content. Triller's editing tools and features make it easy to produce high-quality videos. Brands can use Triller to create visually appealing and entertaining content, leveraging music and trends to engage with their audience. To succeed on Triller, stay updated on the latest trends, collaborate with influencers, and produce content that is both creative and authentic.

Byte created by one of the co-founders of Vine, is a short-form video platform that aims to bring back the charm of Vine's six-second videos. Brands can use Byte to create quick, engaging content that captures the audience's attention. The platform's emphasis on creativity and brevity makes it ideal for brands looking to experiment with new content formats and engage with a younger audience. To thrive on Byte, focus on creating entertaining, shareable content that stands out in the feed.

emerging social media platforms offer unique opportunities for brands to reach new audiences, experiment with innovative content formats, and stay ahead of the competition. Embrace these platforms by creating engaging, high-quality content and actively participating in the unique culture of each platform to maximize your marketing success.

3.10 Integrating Multi-Platform Campaigns

Integrating multi-platform campaigns is a strategic approach that ensures your brand's message is consistent, cohesive, and reaches a broader audience across various social media channels. Here's how to effectively integrate multi-platform campaigns.

Develop a Unified Strategy: Start by defining the overall goals and objectives of your campaign. What are you aiming to achieve? Whether it's brand awareness, lead generation, or customer engagement, having a clear goal helps in crafting a unified strategy that aligns across all platforms. Identify key messages and themes that will resonate with your audience and ensure they are consistent across all channels.

Understand Each Platform's Strengths: Each social media platform has its unique features, audience demographics, and content preferences. For instance, Instagram is ideal for visually-driven content, LinkedIn is best for professional and B2B marketing, while Twitter excels at real-time updates and conversations. Tailor your content to fit the strengths of each platform while maintaining the core message of your campaign. This approach ensures that your content is engaging and relevant to the specific audience of each platform.

Create Platform-Specific Content: While your campaign's core message should be consistent, the execution should be tailored to each platform. For example, you might create a behind-the-scenes video for Instagram Stories, an in-depth article for LinkedIn, a series of tweets for Twitter, and a tutorial video for YouTube. Each piece of content should be optimized for the platform it's intended for, taking into account the format, length, and engagement style preferred by its users.

Leverage Cross-Promotion: Promote your content across multiple platforms to maximize reach and engagement. For instance, share your YouTube videos on Facebook and Twitter, promote your Instagram posts on your LinkedIn page, and encourage your Twitter followers to check out your blog. Cross-promotion not only helps in driving traffic between platforms but also ensures that your audience is aware of your presence across different channels.

Use Consistent Branding: Ensure that your branding is consistent across all platforms. This includes using the same logos, color schemes, and tone of voice. Consistent branding helps in creating a cohesive identity that your audience can recognize and trust, regardless of where they encounter your content.

Track Performance Across Platforms: Use analytics tools to monitor the performance of your campaign on each platform. Platforms like Facebook, Instagram, Twitter, and LinkedIn offer their own analytics, but using a comprehensive tool like Google Analytics or a social media management platform can provide a holistic view of your campaign's performance. Track key metrics such as engagement, reach, click-through rates, and conversions to understand which platforms and content types are driving the best results.

Engage with Your Audience: Active engagement is crucial for the success of any social media campaign. Respond to comments, participate in discussions, and show appreciation for user-generated content. Engagement fosters a sense of community and loyalty, encouraging your audience to interact more with your content and share it with their networks.

Adapt and Optimize: Be flexible and ready to adapt your strategy based on the performance data and audience feedback. If certain content types or platforms are performing exceptionally well, consider allocating more resources to them. Conversely, if some aspects of the campaign are not delivering the expected results, analyze the data to understand why and make necessary adjustments.

Coordinate with Influencers and Partners: Collaborate with influencers and partners who can help amplify your campaign across multiple platforms. Influencers with a presence on various social media channels can bring their followers to your campaign, increasing its reach and impact. Ensure that their content and messaging align with your campaign's goals and branding.

Maintain a Content Calendar: A well-organized content calendar helps in planning and scheduling your posts across different platforms. It ensures that your content is distributed evenly, avoiding overlaps and gaps. A content calendar also allows you to coordinate timely posts that align with key dates and events related to your campaign.

integrating multi-platform campaigns involves creating a cohesive strategy that leverages the strengths of each social media channel. This approach ensures that your brand's message is amplified across multiple touchpoints, driving greater engagement and achieving your marketing objectives.

CHAPTER 4:
INTRODUCTION TO
PAID SOCIAL MEDIA
ADVERTISING

Paid social media advertising has become an indispensable component of modern marketing strategies, providing brands with the ability to reach targeted audiences, boost engagement, and drive conversions effectively. Unlike organic social media efforts, which rely on unpaid methods to grow and engage an audience, paid social media advertising involves investing in various ad formats and campaigns to achieve specific business goals. This section introduces the fundamental concepts and benefits of paid social media advertising, setting the stage for more detailed discussions on platform-specific strategies and best practices.

The Evolution of Paid Social Media Advertising: Over the past decade, social media platforms have transformed from simple networking sites into sophisticated marketing ecosystems. The introduction of paid advertising features on platforms like Facebook, Instagram, Twitter, LinkedIn, and newer entrants like TikTok has revolutionized the way businesses interact with their audience. These platforms offer a variety of ad formats, targeting options, and analytics tools, enabling brands to create highly customized and effective marketing campaigns.

Benefits of Paid Social Media Advertising: Paid social media advertising offers numerous advantages that can enhance your marketing efforts. First and foremost, it provides unparalleled targeting capabilities. Platforms like Facebook and LinkedIn allow advertisers to target users based on demographics, interests, behaviors, and even job titles. This precision targeting ensures that your ads reach the most relevant audience, maximizing the return on investment (ROI). Additionally, paid social media ads can significantly increase brand visibility and awareness, especially when breaking into new markets or launching new products.

Cost-Effectiveness and Flexibility: One of the key benefits of paid social media advertising is its cost-effectiveness. Advertisers can set their budgets and bids, controlling how much they spend on each campaign. Whether you have a small or large budget, paid social media ads can be tailored to fit your financial constraints while still achieving meaningful results. Moreover, the flexibility of ad formats and bidding options allows businesses to adjust their strategies in real-time based on performance data.

Types of Paid Social Media Ads: Various ad formats are available on social media platforms, each designed to achieve different marketing objectives. Common types include:

- Display Ads: Static or dynamic images that appear in users' feeds or sidebars.
- Video Ads: Engaging video content that can be used for storytelling, product demonstrations, or brand messages.
- Carousel Ads: Multiple images or videos within a single ad that users can swipe through.
- Sponsored Posts: Promoted content that appears organically in users' feeds but is marked as sponsored.
- Story Ads: Full-screen vertical ads that appear between

users' stories on platforms like Instagram and Snapchat.

- Lead Generation Ads: Ads designed to capture user information, such as email addresses, directly within the platform.

Measuring Success and ROI: Effective paid social media advertising requires continuous monitoring and optimization. Platforms provide comprehensive analytics tools that allow advertisers to track key performance indicators (KPIs) such as click-through rates (CTR), conversion rates, engagement levels, and cost per acquisition (CPA).

Challenges and Considerations: While paid social media advertising offers significant benefits, it also comes with challenges. Ad fatigue, where users become desensitized to ads, can reduce effectiveness over time. Additionally, the competitive landscape means that advertisers must continuously innovate and refine their strategies to stand out. Privacy concerns and changes in platform algorithms can also impact ad performance and targeting capabilities.

Paid social media advertising is a powerful tool for reaching targeted audiences, enhancing brand visibility, and driving business growth. The following sections will delve deeper into platform-specific strategies and best practices, providing a comprehensive guide to mastering paid social media advertising.

4.2 Setting Up and Managing Facebook Ads

Setting up and managing Facebook Ads involves a series of strategic steps that allow businesses to create effective advertising campaigns, reach targeted audiences, and achieve their marketing goals. With its extensive targeting options, diverse ad formats, and robust analytics, Facebook Ads is a powerful platform for driving engagement and conversions. This section provides a comprehensive guide to setting up and managing Facebook Ads effectively.

Creating a Facebook Business Manager Account: The first step in setting up Facebook Ads is to create a Facebook Business

Manager account. This tool centralizes all of your Facebook marketing activities, allowing you to manage your ad accounts, pages, and team members from one place. To get started, go to business.facebook.com and follow the prompts to set up your Business Manager account.

Setting Up Your Ad Account: Once your Business Manager account is ready, you'll need to set up an ad account. This involves entering your business details, payment information, and time zone. The ad account is where you'll create, manage, and analyze your Facebook ad campaigns.

Defining Your Campaign Objective: Facebook Ads allows you to choose from various campaign objectives, each designed to achieve different marketing goals. The objectives are grouped into three categories: Awareness, Consideration, and Conversion. For example:

- Awareness: Brand Awareness, Reach
- Consideration: Traffic, Engagement, App Installs, Video Views, Lead Generation, Messages
- Conversion: Conversions, Catalog Sales, Store Traffic Select the objective that aligns with your campaign goals to ensure your ads are optimized for the desired outcome.

Targeting Your Audience: One of the most powerful features of Facebook Ads is its advanced targeting options. You can target users based on demographics (age, gender, location), interests (hobbies, activities), behaviors (purchase behavior, device usage), and even life events (anniversaries, birthdays). Custom Audiences allow you to target users who have already interacted with your business, such as website visitors or email subscribers. Lookalike Audiences help you reach new users who are similar to your existing customers.

Choosing Ad Placements: Facebook offers several ad placement options, including Facebook News Feed, Instagram, Audience Network, Messenger, and Stories. You can select automatic placements, where Facebook optimizes the delivery across all placements, or manual placements, where you choose specific locations. Automatic placements are recommended for maximizing reach and performance.

Setting Your Budget and Schedule: Determine your budget and schedule for your ad campaign. You can choose between a daily budget (the amount you're willing to spend per day) and a lifetime budget (the total amount you're willing to spend over the campaign's duration). Additionally, you can set start and end dates for your campaign or run it continuously. Facebook also allows you to schedule ads to run at specific times of the day or week.

Creating Your Ad Creative: The ad creative is the visual and textual content of your ad. Facebook offers various ad formats, including:

- Image Ads: Single image with text and a call-to-action button.
- Video Ads: Short videos that capture attention and tell a story.
- Carousel Ads: Multiple images or videos in a single ad that users can swipe through.
- Slideshow Ads: Lightweight videos created from a series of images.
- Collection Ads: A primary video or image with multiple smaller images below.
- Instant Experience Ads: Full-screen interactive ad format that opens upon clicking. Craft compelling ad creatives that are visually appealing, include a clear call-to-action (CTA), and align with your campaign objective.

Setting Up Tracking and Conversion Tracking: Facebook Pixel is a piece of code that you place on your website to track conversions, optimize ads, and build remarketing audiences. Setting up the Facebook Pixel is crucial for measuring the effectiveness of your campaigns and understanding user behavior. Ensure that the Pixel is correctly installed and configured to track key events such as page views, add to cart, and purchases.

Launching and Monitoring Your Campaign: Once everything is set up, review your ad campaign settings and launch it. After your campaign is live, use Facebook Ads Manager to monitor its performance. Key metrics to track include reach, impressions, click-through rate (CTR), conversion rate, and return on ad spend (ROAS). Facebook Ads Manager provides detailed insights and reports, allowing you to analyze the performance of your ads and make data-driven adjustments.

Optimizing Your Campaigns: Based on the performance data, continuously optimize your campaigns to improve results. This might involve adjusting your targeting, tweaking your ad creatives, experimenting with different ad formats, or reallocating your budget. A/B testing, or split testing, is an effective way to compare different versions of your ads to determine which performs better.

setting up and managing Facebook Ads requires careful planning, strategic execution, and ongoing optimization. The following sections will delve deeper into specific strategies and best practices for maximizing the impact of your Facebook ad campaigns.

4.3 Instagram Ads: Stories, Posts, and IGTV

Instagram Ads offer a variety of formats and placements that enable brands to engage their audience with visually compelling content. As a visually-driven platform, Instagram provides opportunities to create immersive and interactive ad experiences through Stories, Posts, and IGTV. Each format has unique advantages and can be strategically used to achieve different marketing objectives. Here's how to set up and manage Instagram Ads effectively.

Instagram Stories Ads: Stories are one of Instagram's most popular features, with over 500 million users engaging with them daily. Stories Ads are full-screen vertical ads that appear between users' Stories and last up to 15 seconds per slide. These ads are highly engaging and can include photos, videos, GIFs, and interactive elements such as polls, quizzes, and swipe-up links for accounts with over 10,000 followers.

- Creating Stories Ads: Focus on creating visually appealing and dynamic content that captures attention quickly. Use bold visuals, clear messaging, and a strong call-to-action (CTA) to encourage interaction. Leverage interactive features to boost engagement and drive conversions. For example, a fashion brand could use a swipe-up link to direct users to a new collection.

- Targeting and Placement: Utilize Instagram's advanced targeting options to reach your desired audience. Stories Ads can be set up through Facebook Ads Manager, allowing for precise targeting based on demographics, interests, behaviors, and more. Use automatic placements to let Instagram optimize delivery across Stories and other formats for maximum reach and efficiency.

Instagram Feed Posts Ads: Feed Posts Ads appear in users' main Instagram feed and look similar to organic posts, but are marked as sponsored. They can include single images, carousels with multiple images or videos, and video posts up to 60 seconds long. These ads are ideal for driving awareness, engagement, and traffic to your website or app.

- Creating Feed Posts Ads: Ensure your ad creative is high-quality and consistent with your brand's aesthetic. Use captivating visuals and concise, compelling captions. Include a clear CTA, such as "Learn More," "Shop Now," or "Sign Up," to guide users toward your desired action. Carousels are particularly effective for showcasing multiple products or telling a story through a sequence of images.

- Targeting and Placement: Use Instagram's targeting capabilities to reach specific audience segments. Feed Posts Ads can be set up and managed through Facebook

Ads Manager, providing access to detailed targeting options and performance analytics. Consider using automatic placements to extend your ad's reach to both Instagram and Facebook feeds.

Instagram IGTV Ads: IGTV allows users to upload long-form video content, providing an excellent platform for in-depth storytelling and engagement. IGTV Ads are typically short videos that appear as previews in users' feeds and encourage viewers to watch the full video on IGTV. These ads are suitable for brands looking to share detailed content, such as tutorials, interviews, and behind-the-scenes footage.

- Creating IGTV Ads: Focus on producing high-quality, engaging videos that hold viewers' attention. The first few seconds are crucial, so start with a strong hook to entice users to continue watching. Ensure the content is relevant and valuable to your audience. Include a CTA at the end of the video to drive further engagement, such as visiting your website or following your Instagram account.

- Targeting and Placement: Set up IGTV Ads through Facebook Ads Manager, utilizing the platform's targeting and analytics tools. Monitor the performance of your ads, focusing on metrics such as views, engagement rates, and audience retention. Use this data to refine your content and targeting strategies.

Optimizing Instagram Ads: To maximize the effectiveness of your Instagram Ads, regularly analyze performance metrics and make data-driven adjustments. Key metrics to monitor include impressions, reach, engagement (likes, comments, shares), click-through rates (CTR), and conversions. A/B testing different ad creatives, formats, and targeting options can help identify what resonates best with your audience.

Budgeting and Scheduling: Allocate your budget based on your campaign goals and the expected ROI from different ad formats. Instagram Ads allow for flexible budgeting options, including daily and lifetime budgets. Schedule your ads to run at times when your audience is most active to increase visibility and engagement.

Utilizing Influencer Partnerships: Collaborating with influencers can amplify the reach and impact of your Instagram Ads. Influencers with established followings and high engagement rates can help promote your brand authentically. Sponsored posts or Stories created in partnership with influencers can drive significant traffic and conversions.

Leveraging Analytics and Insights: Instagram's analytics tools, available through Facebook Ads Manager, provide valuable insights into the performance of your ads. Use these insights to understand your audience's behavior, identify successful content strategies, and optimize your campaigns. Pay attention to trends in engagement and conversion rates to continuously improve your ad effectiveness.

Instagram Ads offer versatile and powerful formats for engaging with your audience through Stories, Posts, and IGTV.

4.4 Twitter Ads: Promoted Tweets and Trends

Twitter Ads offer unique opportunities for brands to engage with a global audience in real-time through Promoted Tweets, Promoted Trends, and other ad formats. Twitter's fast-paced environment makes it an ideal platform for sharing timely updates, participating in trending conversations, and driving brand awareness. This section explores how to set up and manage Twitter Ads effectively, focusing on Promoted Tweets and Promoted Trends.

Promoted Tweets: Promoted Tweets are regular tweets that advertisers pay to display to a broader audience beyond their followers. These tweets appear in users' timelines, search results, and on profiles, marked as "Promoted" to differentiate them from organic tweets. Promoted Tweets can include text, images, videos, and links, making them versatile for various marketing objectives.

- Creating Promoted Tweets: Start by crafting engaging

and concise tweets that capture attention quickly. Use strong visuals, compelling copy, and clear calls-to-action (CTAs) to encourage interaction. Ensure your tweets are relevant and timely, aligning with current events or trends that resonate with your audience. For example, a tech company might promote a tweet about a new product launch coinciding with a major tech conference.

- Targeting and Placement: Utilize Twitter's advanced targeting options to reach specific demographics, interests, behaviors, and geographic locations. You can also target users based on keywords, hashtags, and user engagement with similar accounts. Twitter's targeting capabilities allow you to hone in on your ideal audience, ensuring your Promoted Tweets reach the most relevant users.

Promoted Trends: Promoted Trends are topics that appear at the top of the "Trends for You" section on Twitter, giving them high visibility. This ad format is ideal for creating buzz around major events, product launches, or brand campaigns. Promoted Trends typically run for 24 hours, providing a concentrated period of heightened awareness and engagement.

- Creating Promoted Trends: Select a hashtag or keyword that encapsulates your campaign and encourages user participation. Ensure the trend is catchy, relevant, and easy to remember. Alongside your Promoted Trend, consider using Promoted Tweets to provide additional context and drive engagement. For example, a movie studio might use a Promoted Trend to generate excitement for a new film release, accompanied by Promoted Tweets with trailers and behind-the-scenes content.

- Maximizing Engagement: Encourage users to engage with your Promoted Trend by creating interactive content, such as polls, quizzes, or contests. Leverage influencers and brand ambassadors to amplify the trend and drive further engagement. Monitoring the conversation and actively participating in real-time can help maintain momentum and foster a sense of community.

Setting Up Twitter Ads: To set up Twitter Ads, start by creating a Twitter Ads account. Access the Twitter Ads Manager to create and manage your campaigns. Choose your campaign objective based on your marketing goals, such as awareness, engagement, website clicks, app installs, or video views. Twitter's campaign objectives guide the ad creation process and optimize your ads for the desired outcomes.

- Budgeting and Bidding: Determine your budget and bid strategy. Twitter offers flexible budgeting options, including daily and total campaign budgets. Choose between automatic bidding, where Twitter optimizes your bid for the best results, or manual bidding, where you set your maximum bid for specific actions. Monitor your spending and adjust your budget as needed to maximize ROI.

- Ad Formats: In addition to Promoted Tweets and Promoted Trends, Twitter offers other ad formats like Promoted Accounts (to gain followers) and Promoted Moments (curated stories combining multiple tweets). Select the ad format that best aligns with your campaign objectives and complements your overall strategy.

Analyzing Performance and Optimization: Use Twitter Analytics to track the performance of your ads. Key metrics to monitor include impressions, engagement rates, click-through rates (CTR), conversions, and cost per engagement (CPE). Analyzing these metrics provides insights into what's working and what needs adjustment.

- A/B Testing: Conduct A/B testing by running different versions of your Promoted Tweets or targeting different audience segments. Compare the performance to identify the most effective strategies and optimize your campaigns accordingly. Testing variables such as ad copy, images, CTAs, and targeting options can help refine your approach and improve results.

- Engagement and Interaction: Engage with users who interact with your Promoted Tweets and Trends. Responding to comments, retweeting user-generated content, and participating in relevant conversations can enhance your brand's presence and foster a positive relationship with your audience.

Leveraging Real-Time Marketing: Twitter's real-time nature makes it ideal for live events, breaking news, and timely promotions. Plan your Promoted Tweets and Trends to coincide with relevant events or trending topics to maximize visibility and engagement. For instance, a sports brand might promote tweets during a major sports event or a retail brand might use Promoted Trends during Black Friday sales.

Twitter Ads offer versatile and effective options for promoting your brand, engaging with a broader audience, and driving campaign success.

4.5 LinkedIn Ads: Sponsored Content and InMail

LinkedIn Ads provide a powerful platform for B2B marketers and professionals to reach a highly targeted audience. With its focus on professional networking and industry-specific content, LinkedIn offers unique ad formats that cater to business audiences. This section explores how to set up and manage LinkedIn Ads effectively, focusing on Sponsored Content and Sponsored InMail.

Sponsored Content: Sponsored Content appears directly in the LinkedIn feed, blending seamlessly with organic posts. This ad format includes single image ads, carousel ads, and video ads, offering versatility to achieve various marketing objectives such as brand awareness, lead generation, and engagement.

- Creating Sponsored Content: Start by defining your campaign objective—whether it's increasing brand awareness, driving website traffic, or generating leads. Craft high-quality, professional content that resonates with LinkedIn's professional audience. Use compelling visuals, clear and concise copy, and strong calls-to-action (CTAs). For example, an IT services company might create a video ad showcasing a new software solution, with a CTA to download a free trial.

- Targeting and Placement: LinkedIn's robust targeting options allow you to reach specific professional demographics, including job titles, industries, company sizes, and seniority levels. Utilize LinkedIn's audience targeting features to ensure your Sponsored Content reaches the most relevant audience. You can also create Custom Audiences based on website visitors, email contacts, and lookalike audiences to refine your targeting further.

Sponsored InMail: Sponsored InMail is a unique LinkedIn ad format that delivers personalized messages directly to users' LinkedIn inboxes. This format is highly effective for direct engagement, making it ideal for lead generation, event invitations, and personalized offers.

- Creating Sponsored InMail: Craft personalized and relevant messages that address the recipient's needs or interests. Use a clear and engaging subject line to encourage opens, and keep the body of the message concise and action-oriented. Include a strong CTA, such as "Register for our webinar" or "Download our whitepaper," to drive conversions. For instance, a marketing firm might use Sponsored InMail to invite senior marketing executives to an exclusive industry webinar.

- Targeting and Delivery: LinkedIn ensures that Sponsored InMail messages are only delivered when users are active, increasing the likelihood of engagement. Use LinkedIn's targeting options to send messages to specific professional segments, ensuring relevance and personalization. Segment your audience based on job roles, industries, or company sizes to tailor your messages effectively.

Setting Up LinkedIn Ads: To set up LinkedIn Ads, start by creating a LinkedIn Campaign Manager account. Choose your campaign objective, such as brand awareness, website visits, engagement, video views, lead generation, or job applications. LinkedIn's guided campaign setup process helps you select the appropriate ad format and targeting options.

- Budgeting and Bidding: Set your budget and bid strategy according to your campaign goals. LinkedIn offers daily and total budget options, as well as bid strategies like cost-per-click (CPC), cost-per-impression (CPM), and cost-per-send (CPS) for Sponsored InMail. Monitor your spending and adjust your bids to optimize performance and maximize ROI.

- Ad Formats: Besides Sponsored Content and Sponsored InMail, LinkedIn offers other ad formats such as Text Ads (simple ads that appear on the sidebar), Dynamic Ads (personalized ads that feature the user's profile data), and Video Ads. Select the ad format that aligns with your campaign objectives and complements your overall strategy.

Analyzing Performance and Optimization: Use LinkedIn's analytics tools to track the performance of your ads. Key metrics to monitor include impressions, clicks, click-through rates (CTR), conversions, and cost per conversion. LinkedIn Campaign Manager provides detailed insights into ad performance, helping you understand what's working and what needs adjustment.

- A/B Testing: Conduct A/B testing to compare different versions of your ads, targeting options, and CTAs. Testing variables such as ad copy, images, CTAs, and audience segments can help identify the most effective strategies. Use the insights from A/B testing to optimize your campaigns for better results.

- Engagement and Interaction: Engage with users who interact with your ads by responding to comments, messages, and connections. Building relationships and fostering engagement can enhance your brand's presence and credibility on LinkedIn.

Leveraging LinkedIn's Professional Network: LinkedIn's professional network is a valuable asset for B2B marketers. Use Sponsored Content and Sponsored InMail to reach decision-makers, industry leaders, and potential clients. Participate in LinkedIn Groups, share valuable content, and engage with industry discussions to build your brand's authority and network.

Utilizing Lead Generation Forms: LinkedIn's Lead Gen Forms simplify the process of capturing leads directly within the platform. These forms auto-populate with users' LinkedIn profile data, making it easy for users to submit their information. Use Lead Gen Forms in your Sponsored Content and Sponsored InMail campaigns to drive high-quality leads and streamline the conversion process.

LinkedIn Ads offer powerful tools for B2B marketers to reach and engage with a professional audience.

4.6 YouTube Ads: Video Ads and Display Ads

YouTube Ads offer a powerful way to reach a vast audience through engaging video content and strategically placed display ads. As the second largest search engine in the world, YouTube provides a unique platform for brands to connect with viewers in a dynamic and impactful manner. This section explores how to set up and manage YouTube Ads effectively, focusing on Video Ads and Display Ads.

Video Ads: YouTube Video Ads come in various formats, each designed to achieve different marketing objectives, such as increasing brand awareness, driving traffic, or boosting conversions. The primary types of video ads on YouTube are TrueView Ads, Non-Skippable Ads, and Bumper Ads.

- TrueView Ads: TrueView Ads are the most common type of YouTube video ads, allowing viewers to choose whether to watch the ad. They are skippable after 5 seconds and advertisers only pay when viewers watch at least 30 seconds, the entire ad, or engage with the ad (such as clicking a call-to-action).
  - In-Stream Ads: These ads play before, during, or after other videos and can be up to 3 minutes long, though shorter ads are generally more effective.
  - Discovery Ads: These ads appear alongside

YouTube search results, related videos, and on the YouTube homepage. They consist of a thumbnail image and text, enticing viewers to click and watch.

- Creating TrueView Ads: Focus on creating engaging content that captures attention within the first 5 seconds. Use strong visuals, clear messaging, and compelling CTAs to encourage viewers to take action. For instance, a travel company might use in-stream ads to showcase breathtaking destinations, inviting viewers to explore travel packages on their website.

- Non-Skippable Ads: These ads must be watched before the viewer can proceed to their desired video. They can be up to 15-20 seconds long and are ideal for delivering a concise, impactful message.
  - Creating Non-Skippable Ads: Make every second count by delivering a clear and memorable message quickly. Use strong visuals and a direct CTA to drive engagement. For example, a tech company could use non-skippable ads to highlight the key features of a new product launch.

- Bumper Ads: These are non-skippable ads up to 6 seconds long. They are designed to increase brand awareness and reach by delivering a short, impactful message.
  - Creating Bumper Ads: Focus on a single, powerful message or brand element. Keep the visuals and text simple yet compelling. For example, a beverage brand might use bumper ads to promote a new flavor, using eye-catching visuals and a catchy tagline.

Display Ads: YouTube Display Ads are another effective way to reach viewers through visually engaging content. These ads appear alongside video content and can include text, images, and interactive elements.

- Overlay Ads: These are semi-transparent ads that appear on the lower portion of the video. They can include text or images and a CTA, driving traffic to your website or landing page.

- ◦ Creating Overlay Ads: Ensure your overlay ads are unobtrusive yet noticeable. Use concise, compelling text and a clear CTA. For example, an e-commerce brand could use overlay ads to promote a limited-time discount.

- . Banner Ads: These ads appear on the right sidebar of the YouTube homepage, channel pages, and video pages. They can include images, text, and CTAs.
  - ◦ Creating Banner Ads: Design visually appealing banners that align with your brand's aesthetic. Use bold text and strong CTAs to capture attention and drive clicks. For example, a fitness brand might use banner ads to advertise a new workout program.

Setting Up YouTube Ads: To set up YouTube Ads, start by creating a Google Ads account if you don't already have one. Link your YouTube channel to your Google Ads account to manage your campaigns.

- . Choosing Your Campaign Objective: Select a campaign objective that aligns with your marketing goals, such as brand awareness, lead generation, website traffic, or sales.

- . Targeting Your Audience: Utilize YouTube's advanced targeting options to reach specific demographics, interests, behaviors, and geographic locations. You can also create Custom Audiences based on website visitors, customer lists, or app users to refine your targeting.

- . Bidding and Budgeting: Set your budget and bid strategy according to your campaign goals. Google Ads offers various bidding options, such as cost-per-view (CPV), cost-per-click (CPC), and cost-per-thousand-impressions (CPM). Monitor your spending and adjust your bids to optimize performance.

Analyzing Performance and Optimization: Use YouTube Analytics and Google Ads reports to track the performance of your ads. Key metrics to monitor include views, view-through rates (VTR), engagement, clicks, conversions, and cost per conversion.

- A/B Testing: Conduct A/B testing by running different versions of your video and display ads. Test variables such as ad creative, length, CTAs, and targeting options to identify the most effective strategies.
- Optimizing Campaigns: Based on performance data, optimize your campaigns by adjusting targeting, refining ad creatives, and reallocating budget to the best-performing ads.

Engaging with Your Audience: Engage with viewers by responding to comments on your videos and encouraging interaction. Building a community around your content can enhance brand loyalty and drive further engagement.

Leveraging YouTube's Features: Utilize YouTube's features such as end screens and cards to add interactive elements to your videos. These features can promote other videos, encourage subscriptions, and drive traffic to your website or landing pages.

YouTube Ads offer diverse and powerful formats for engaging with a vast audience through video and display content.

4.7 Pinterest Ads: Promoted Pins and Shopping Ads

Pinterest Ads provide a unique opportunity for brands to reach users who are actively seeking inspiration and ideas. With its visual and discovery-driven nature, Pinterest is ideal for showcasing products, driving traffic, and boosting sales. This section explores how to set up and manage Pinterest Ads effectively, focusing on Promoted Pins and Shopping Ads.

Promoted Pins: Promoted Pins are standard Pins that advertisers pay to promote, ensuring they reach a wider audience. These ads blend seamlessly with organic content, appearing in users' home feeds, category feeds, and search results.

- Creating Promoted Pins: Start by selecting high-quality

images or videos that are visually appealing and relevant to your target audience. Write clear, engaging descriptions that include relevant keywords to improve discoverability. Use strong calls-to-action (CTAs) to encourage users to click through to your website or landing page. For example, a home decor brand might promote Pins featuring beautifully styled rooms with a CTA like "Shop the Look."

- Targeting and Placement: Utilize Pinterest's advanced targeting options to reach specific demographics, interests, keywords, and behaviors. You can also create Custom Audiences based on website visitors, customer lists, and engagement with your Pins. Pinterest's targeting features allow you to refine your audience, ensuring your Promoted Pins reach the most relevant users.

Shopping Ads: Shopping Ads on Pinterest allow users to browse and purchase products directly from your Pins. These ads are designed to showcase products with pricing and availability information, making it easy for users to shop directly from the platform.

- Creating Shopping Ads: Start by setting up your product catalog in Pinterest's Catalogs feature. This involves uploading a data feed with information about your products, including images, descriptions, prices, and availability. Once your catalog is set up, you can create Shopping Ads that feature individual products or collections. Ensure your product images are high-quality and your descriptions are detailed and accurate. For example, a fashion retailer might create Shopping Ads showcasing the latest seasonal styles.

- Targeting and Placement: Use Pinterest's targeting options to reach users who are most likely to be interested in your products. Shopping Ads can be targeted based on demographics, interests, and behaviors, as well as engagement with your previous Pins. Leverage Dynamic Retargeting to reach users who have already shown interest in your products by visiting your website or engaging with your Pins.

Setting Up Pinterest Ads: To set up Pinterest Ads, start by creating a Pinterest Business account if you don't already have one. Access the Pinterest Ads Manager to create and manage your campaigns.

- Choosing Your Campaign Objective: Select a campaign objective that aligns with your marketing goals, such as brand awareness, traffic, or conversions. Pinterest offers specific campaign objectives to help optimize your ads for the desired outcomes.

- Budgeting and Bidding: Determine your budget and bid strategy based on your campaign goals. Pinterest offers flexible budgeting options, including daily and lifetime budgets, as well as automatic and custom bidding strategies. Monitor your spending and adjust your bids to optimize performance and maximize ROI.

Analyzing Performance and Optimization: Use Pinterest Analytics to track the performance of your ads. Key metrics to monitor include impressions, saves, clicks, click-through rates (CTR), and conversions. Pinterest Analytics provides insights into how users interact with your Pins and Shopping Ads, helping you understand what works and what needs adjustment.

- A/B Testing: Conduct A/B testing by running different versions of your Promoted Pins and Shopping Ads. Test variables such as ad creative, descriptions, CTAs, and targeting options to identify the most effective strategies. Use the insights from A/B testing to optimize your campaigns for better results.

- Optimizing Campaigns: Based on performance data, continuously optimize your campaigns by refining targeting, adjusting ad creatives, and reallocating budget to the best-performing ads. Focus on improving key metrics such as CTR and conversion rates to maximize the effectiveness of your Pinterest Ads.

Engaging with Your Audience: Engage with users who interact with your Promoted Pins and Shopping Ads by responding to comments and encouraging further interaction. Building a community around your content can enhance brand loyalty and drive additional engagement.

Leveraging Pinterest's Features: Utilize Pinterest's features such as Rich Pins and Buyable Pins to enhance your ads. Rich Pins provide extra information directly on the Pin, such as pricing and availability, making them more informative and actionable. Buyable Pins allow users to purchase products directly from Pinterest, streamlining the shopping experience.

Pinterest Ads offer a visually engaging and effective way to reach users who are actively seeking inspiration and ideas.

4.8 TikTok Ads: In-Feed Ads and Branded Hashtag Challenges

TikTok has quickly become one of the most influential social media platforms, particularly among younger audiences. Its short-form, video-centric format offers unique opportunities for brands to create engaging and viral content. This section explores how to set up and manage TikTok Ads effectively, focusing on In-Feed Ads and Branded Hashtag Challenges.

In-Feed Ads: In-Feed Ads are native ads that appear in the "For You" feed as users scroll through content. These ads blend seamlessly with user-generated content, making them less intrusive and more engaging.

- Creating In-Feed Ads: Focus on creating high-quality, attention-grabbing videos that align with the style and tone of popular TikTok content. Use strong visuals, engaging music, and clear calls-to-action (CTAs) to encourage interaction. The first few seconds are crucial, so ensure your message is clear and captivating from the start. For example, a beauty brand might create a tutorial video showcasing a new makeup product with a CTA to "Shop Now."

- Targeting and Placement: Utilize TikTok's advanced targeting options to reach specific demographics, interests, and behaviors. You can also create Custom Audiences based on website visitors, customer lists, or app users to refine your targeting further. TikTok's targeting capabilities ensure that your In-Feed Ads reach the most relevant audience, maximizing engagement and conversions.

Branded Hashtag Challenges: Branded Hashtag Challenges encourage users to create and share content based on a specific hashtag, often involving a challenge or theme. These challenges can quickly go viral, generating significant user engagement and brand visibility.

- Creating Branded Hashtag Challenges: Develop a creative and engaging challenge that resonates with TikTok's audience. Choose a catchy, memorable hashtag and create a launch video that explains the challenge and encourages participation. Partnering with popular TikTok influencers can amplify your challenge and drive higher engagement. For example, a fitness brand might launch a workout challenge with a hashtag like #FitWithUs, encouraging users to share their workout routines.

- Maximizing Engagement: Promote your Branded Hashtag Challenge through In-Feed Ads and collaborations with influencers. Encourage users to participate by offering incentives such as prizes or featuring the best submissions on your brand's TikTok page. Actively engage with participants by liking, commenting, and sharing their content to foster a sense of community and excitement around the challenge.

Setting Up TikTok Ads: To set up TikTok Ads, start by creating a TikTok Ads Manager account. This platform allows you to create, manage, and analyze your ad campaigns.

- Choosing Your Campaign Objective: Select a campaign objective that aligns with your marketing goals, such as brand awareness, website traffic, app installs, or conversions. TikTok offers specific campaign objectives to help optimize your ads for the desired outcomes.

- Budgeting and Bidding: Determine your budget and bid strategy based on your campaign goals. TikTok offers flexible budgeting options, including daily and total budgets, as well as automatic and manual bidding strategies. Monitor your spending and adjust your bids to optimize performance and maximize ROI.

Analyzing Performance and Optimization: Use TikTok Analytics to track the performance of your ads. Key metrics to monitor include views, likes, shares, comments, click-through rates (CTR), and conversions. TikTok Analytics provides insights into how users interact with your In-Feed Ads and Branded Hashtag Challenges, helping you understand what works and what needs adjustment.

- A/B Testing: Conduct A/B testing by running different versions of your ads. Test variables such as ad creative, video length, music, CTAs, and targeting options to identify the most effective strategies. Use the insights from A/B testing to optimize your campaigns for better results.

- Optimizing Campaigns: Based on performance data, continuously optimize your campaigns by refining targeting, adjusting ad creatives, and reallocating budget to the best-performing ads. Focus on improving key metrics such as engagement rates and conversion rates to maximize the effectiveness of your TikTok Ads.

Engaging with Your Audience: Engage with users who interact with your In-Feed Ads and Branded Hashtag Challenges by responding to comments, liking user-generated content, and encouraging further interaction. Building a community around your content can enhance brand loyalty and drive additional engagement.

Leveraging TikTok's Features: Utilize TikTok's creative tools and features to enhance your ads. TikTok offers a range of effects, filters, and editing tools that can make your content more engaging and visually appealing. Collaborate with TikTok influencers to leverage their creative expertise and reach their followers.

Cross-Promoting TikTok Content: Promote your TikTok content on other social media platforms to increase visibility and engagement. Share your TikTok videos on Instagram, Twitter, Facebook, and other channels to attract a broader audience and encourage them to follow your TikTok account.

TikTok Ads offer a dynamic and engaging way to reach a young, active audience through In-Feed Ads and Branded Hashtag Challenges.

4.9 Snapchat Ads: Snap Ads and Sponsored Lenses

Snapchat Ads provide an engaging and immersive way for brands to connect with a younger audience through creative and interactive content. With its emphasis on real-time, ephemeral content, Snapchat offers unique advertising formats that can drive high engagement and brand awareness. This section explores how to set up and manage Snapchat Ads effectively, focusing on Snap Ads and Sponsored Lenses.

Snap Ads: Snap Ads are full-screen vertical video ads that appear between user stories and other content on Snapchat. These ads can be up to 10 seconds long and are designed to be quick, engaging, and easy to consume.

- Creating Snap Ads: Focus on creating visually appealing and concise video content that captures attention within the first few seconds. Use strong visuals, engaging music, and a clear call-to-action (CTA) to encourage interaction. Snap Ads can include interactive elements such as swipe-up links that direct users to your website, app, or landing page. For example, a fashion brand might create a Snap Ad showcasing a new clothing line with a CTA to "Swipe Up to Shop Now."

- Targeting and Placement: Utilize Snapchat's advanced targeting options to reach specific demographics, interests, locations, and behaviors. You can also create Custom Audiences based on customer lists, website visitors, or app users to refine your targeting further. Snapchat's targeting capabilities ensure that your Snap

Ads reach the most relevant audience, maximizing engagement and conversions.

Sponsored Lenses: Sponsored Lenses are augmented reality (AR) experiences that allow users to interact with your brand in a fun and engaging way. These lenses can be used to create branded animations, effects, and interactive elements that users can apply to their photos and videos.

- Creating Sponsored Lenses: Design creative and engaging AR experiences that align with your brand and appeal to Snapchat's audience. Sponsored Lenses should be visually appealing, easy to use, and encourage user interaction. For example, a beverage brand might create a Sponsored Lens that allows users to "pour" a virtual drink into their Snapchat selfies. Collaborating with Snapchat's creative team or third-party developers can help you create high-quality, engaging lenses.

- Maximizing Engagement: Promote your Sponsored Lenses through Snap Ads and influencer collaborations to drive higher engagement. Encourage users to share their creations with their friends, increasing the reach and visibility of your lens. Actively engaging with users who share your lens can foster a sense of community and excitement around your brand.

Setting Up Snapchat Ads: To set up Snapchat Ads, start by creating a Snapchat Ads Manager account. This platform allows you to create, manage, and analyze your ad campaigns.

- Choosing Your Campaign Objective: Select a campaign objective that aligns with your marketing goals, such as brand awareness, website traffic, app installs, or sales. Snapchat offers specific campaign objectives to help optimize your ads for the desired outcomes.

- Budgeting and Bidding: Determine your budget and bid strategy based on your campaign goals. Snapchat offers flexible budgeting options, including daily and total budgets, as well as automatic and manual bidding strategies. Monitor your spending and adjust your bids to optimize performance and maximize ROI.

Analyzing Performance and Optimization: Use Snapchat Analytics to track the performance of your ads. Key metrics to monitor include impressions, swipe-ups, views, engagement rates, and conversions. Snapchat Analytics provides insights into how users interact with your Snap Ads and Sponsored Lenses, helping you understand what works and what needs adjustment.

- A/B Testing: Conduct A/B testing by running different versions of your ads. Test variables such as ad creative, video length, music, CTAs, and targeting options to identify the most effective strategies. Use the insights from A/B testing to optimize your campaigns for better results.

- Optimizing Campaigns: Based on performance data, continuously optimize your campaigns by refining targeting, adjusting ad creatives, and reallocating budget to the best-performing ads. Focus on improving key metrics such as engagement rates and conversion rates to maximize the effectiveness of your Snapchat Ads.

Engaging with Your Audience: Engage with users who interact with your Snap Ads and Sponsored Lenses by responding to comments, sharing user-generated content, and encouraging further interaction. Building a community around your content can enhance brand loyalty and drive additional engagement.

Leveraging Snapchat's Features: Utilize Snapchat's creative tools and features to enhance your ads. Snapchat offers a range of effects, filters, and editing tools that can make your content more engaging and visually appealing. Collaborate with Snapchat influencers to leverage their creative expertise and reach their followers.

Cross-Promoting Snapchat Content: Promote your Snapchat content on other social media platforms to increase visibility and engagement. Share your Snap Ads and Sponsored Lenses on Instagram, Twitter, Facebook, and other channels to attract a broader audience and encourage them to follow your Snapchat account.

Snapchat Ads offer a dynamic and engaging way to reach a young, active audience through Snap Ads and Sponsored Lenses.

4.10 LinkedIn Sponsored Content: Text Ads and Dynamic Ads

LinkedIn Sponsored Content offers powerful tools for B2B marketers and professionals to reach their target audience with precision. As a platform focused on professional networking and industry-specific content, LinkedIn provides unique advertising formats that cater to business audiences. This section explores how to set up and manage LinkedIn Sponsored Content effectively, focusing on Text Ads and Dynamic Ads.

Text Ads: Text Ads are simple yet effective advertisements that appear on the right-hand side or at the top of LinkedIn pages. They typically consist of a short headline, a brief description, and an optional small image. Text Ads are ideal for driving traffic to your website, generating leads, or promoting content downloads.

- Creating Text Ads: Start by crafting a concise and compelling headline that captures attention. Your headline should be relevant to your target audience and clearly convey the value proposition. The description should provide additional context and include a strong call-to-action (CTA), such as "Learn More," "Download Now," or "Sign Up." Including an image can enhance the ad's visibility and engagement, but it's not mandatory. For example, a software company might use a Text Ad to promote a free eBook on industry trends.

- Targeting and Placement: Utilize LinkedIn's advanced targeting options to reach specific professional demographics, including job titles, industries, company sizes, and seniority levels. LinkedIn's targeting capabilities ensure your Text Ads are seen by the most relevant audience, maximizing the likelihood of engagement and conversions.

Dynamic Ads: Dynamic Ads are personalized ads that use LinkedIn member profile data to create a customized experience for each user. These ads can include member names, profile pictures, and other details to make the content more relevant and engaging. Dynamic Ads are ideal for increasing brand awareness, attracting followers, and driving specific actions such as event registrations.

- Creating Dynamic Ads: Design your Dynamic Ads to be visually appealing and personalized. LinkedIn offers several types of Dynamic Ads, including Follower Ads (to increase your follower base), Spotlight Ads (to drive traffic or conversions), and Content Ads (to promote downloads or sign-ups). Customize the ad content to align with your campaign objectives and target audience. For instance, a business consultancy might use Follower Ads to grow its LinkedIn Page followers by featuring a personalized message and the user's profile picture.

- Targeting and Placement: Dynamic Ads leverage LinkedIn's targeting capabilities to reach the most relevant audience. Use the same advanced targeting options available for Text Ads to ensure your Dynamic Ads are seen by professionals who are most likely to engage with your content.

Setting Up LinkedIn Sponsored Content: To set up LinkedIn Sponsored Content, start by creating a LinkedIn Campaign Manager account if you don't already have one. This platform allows you to create, manage, and analyze your ad campaigns.

- Choosing Your Campaign Objective: Select a campaign objective that aligns with your marketing goals, such as brand awareness, website visits, engagement, lead generation, or job applications. LinkedIn offers specific campaign objectives to help optimize your ads for the desired outcomes.

- Budgeting and Bidding: Determine your budget and bid strategy based on your campaign goals. LinkedIn offers flexible budgeting options, including daily and total budgets, as well as automatic and manual bidding strategies. Monitor your spending and adjust your bids to optimize performance and maximize ROI.

Analyzing Performance and Optimization: Use LinkedIn

Analytics to track the performance of your ads. Key metrics to monitor include impressions, clicks, click-through rates (CTR), engagement, conversions, and cost per conversion. LinkedIn Analytics provides insights into how users interact with your Text Ads and Dynamic Ads, helping you understand what works and what needs adjustment.

- A/B Testing: Conduct A/B testing by running different versions of your ads. Test variables such as ad copy, images, CTAs, and targeting options to identify the most effective strategies. Use the insights from A/B testing to optimize your campaigns for better results.

- Optimizing Campaigns: Based on performance data, continuously optimize your campaigns by refining targeting, adjusting ad creatives, and reallocating budget to the best-performing ads. Focus on improving key metrics such as CTR and conversion rates to maximize the effectiveness of your LinkedIn Sponsored Content.

Engaging with Your Audience: Engage with users who interact with your Text Ads and Dynamic Ads by responding to comments, messages, and connections. Building relationships and fostering engagement can enhance your brand's presence and credibility on LinkedIn.

Leveraging LinkedIn's Professional Network: LinkedIn's professional network is a valuable asset for B2B marketers. Use Sponsored Content to reach decision-makers, industry leaders, and potential clients. Participate in LinkedIn Groups, share valuable content, and engage with industry discussions to build your brand's authority and network.

Utilizing Lead Generation Forms: LinkedIn's Lead Gen Forms simplify the process of capturing leads directly within the platform. These forms auto-populate with users' LinkedIn profile data, making it easy for users to submit their information. Use Lead Gen Forms in your Text Ads and Dynamic Ads campaigns to drive high-quality leads and streamline the conversion process.

LinkedIn Sponsored Content offers powerful tools for B2B marketers to reach and engage with a professional audience.

CHAPTER 5: BUILDING AND NURTURING ONLINE COMMUNITIES

B uilding and nurturing online communities is essential for creating a loyal and engaged audience that not only supports your brand but also advocates for it. A vibrant community fosters a sense of belonging among members, encourages meaningful interactions, and provides valuable feedback. To establish a thriving online community, start by identifying your target audience's interests and pain points. Create a welcoming and inclusive environment where members feel valued and heard. Regularly share relevant content that resonates with your community's interests, such as helpful tips, industry news, and behind-the-scenes looks at your brand. Encourage discussions by asking open-ended questions and prompting members to share their experiences and opinions. Active participation from community managers and brand representatives is crucial; respond to comments, acknowledge contributions, and mediate any conflicts to maintain a positive atmosphere. Hosting virtual events, such as webinars, Q&A sessions, and live chats, can further strengthen the community by providing opportunities for real-time interaction. Additionally, recognizing and rewarding active members with shout-outs, exclusive content, or special offers can boost engagement and loyalty.

5.2 Strategies for Consistent Engagement

Consistent engagement is crucial for maintaining a vibrant and active online presence. To keep your audience engaged, it's important to implement strategies that foster regular interaction and create a sense of community. Start by developing a content calendar that outlines your posting schedule, ensuring a steady flow of relevant and diverse content. This might include a mix of informative articles, entertaining videos, inspiring quotes, and interactive polls. Consistency in posting helps to keep your audience interested and coming back for more.

Personalization is another key strategy for driving engagement. Address your audience directly, use their names when possible, and tailor your content to their interests and preferences. Utilize data analytics to understand what type of content resonates most with your audience and adjust your strategy accordingly. Respond promptly to comments, messages, and mentions to show that you value your audience's input and are actively listening. This two-way communication builds trust and encourages further interaction.

Interactive content is particularly effective in boosting engagement. Polls, quizzes, contests, and challenges invite your audience to participate actively rather than passively consuming content. For example, a fitness brand might run a weekly workout challenge encouraging followers to share their progress using a specific hashtag. Such initiatives not only engage your audience but also generate user-generated content, expanding your reach.

Live content, such as live videos or live chats, can create a sense of immediacy and excitement. Hosting live Q&A sessions, product launches, or behind-the-scenes tours can make your audience feel involved and connected to your brand. Encourage viewers to ask questions and interact in real-time to maximize engagement.

Storytelling is another powerful tool for consistent engagement.

Share stories that highlight customer experiences, brand history, or the people behind your products. Stories evoke emotions and make your brand more relatable, fostering a deeper connection with your audience.

Finally, collaborations with influencers or other brands can introduce your content to new audiences and provide fresh, engaging perspectives. Partnering with influencers who align with your brand values can amplify your message and attract new followers.

consistent engagement requires a combination of strategic planning, personalized communication, interactive content, live experiences, compelling storytelling, and strategic collaborations.

5.3 Leveraging User-Generated Content

Leveraging user-generated content (UGC) is a powerful strategy for engaging your audience and building authenticity around your brand. UGC includes any content—such as photos, videos, reviews, and testimonials—created by your customers or followers rather than your brand itself. This type of content not only enhances your marketing efforts but also fosters a sense of community and trust among your audience.

To effectively leverage UGC, start by encouraging your audience to share their experiences with your brand. This can be achieved through social media contests, challenges, and prompts that invite users to post content using specific hashtags. For instance, a beauty brand might ask customers to share their makeup looks using a branded hashtag, providing visibility and a chance to be featured on the brand's official channels. Offering incentives, such as discounts or the opportunity to win prizes, can further motivate participation.

Once you have a collection of UGC, showcase it prominently across your social media platforms, website, and other marketing channels. Highlighting customer photos, videos, and testimonials not only provides social proof but also shows that you value your community's contributions. This recognition can deepen customer loyalty and encourage others to share their content as well.

It's important to engage with the creators of UGC by liking, commenting, and sharing their posts. Acknowledge their contributions and express appreciation to foster a positive relationship. This interaction can turn satisfied customers into brand advocates who are more likely to promote your products to their own networks.

UGC also offers valuable insights into how customers use and perceive your products. Analyzing this content can provide feedback for product development, identify new use cases, and highlight potential areas for improvement. Sharing these insights with your audience can demonstrate that you listen to and act on their feedback, further building trust and loyalty.

When using UGC, always seek permission from the content creators and give them credit. This ethical practice respects their contributions and reinforces the authenticity of your brand. Additionally, consider creating guidelines for UGC to ensure that the content aligns with your brand values and aesthetic.

Incorporating UGC into your marketing strategy can also enhance your content variety and reduce the burden on your content creation team. Authentic customer stories and experiences can resonate more with potential customers than brand-produced content alone.

leveraging user-generated content can significantly enhance engagement, build trust, and create a sense of community around your brand.

5.4 Utilizing Influencer Partnerships

Influencer partnerships have become an integral part of social media marketing, offering brands the opportunity to reach new audiences, build credibility, and drive engagement through the voices of trusted individuals.

To effectively utilize influencer partnerships, start by identifying influencers who align with your brand values and target audience. Look for influencers whose content, style, and followers match your brand's identity and the demographics you aim to reach. Tools like social media analytics platforms and influencer marketing software can help you find and evaluate potential influencers based on their engagement rates, follower demographics, and past collaboration successes.

Once you've identified potential influencers, approach them with a clear and compelling proposal. Highlight the mutual benefits of the partnership, such as increased exposure for the influencer and enhanced brand visibility for your company. Be transparent about your expectations, including deliverables, timelines, and compensation. Influencers appreciate clarity and professionalism, which sets the stage for a successful collaboration.

When working with influencers, allow them creative freedom to ensure the content feels authentic and resonates with their audience. Influencers know what works best for their followers, so their unique voice and style should be preserved in the sponsored content. This authenticity helps build trust and avoids the appearance of overt advertising, which can be off-putting to audiences.

There are several types of influencer collaborations to consider:

- Sponsored Posts: Influencers create and share content featuring your product or service on their social media channels. This can include photos, videos, stories, or blog posts. Ensure the content aligns with your brand message and includes clear CTAs.

- Product Reviews and Unboxings: Influencers provide honest reviews or unboxings of your products. This type of content can drive interest and conversions by showcasing your product's features and benefits from a trusted source.

- Giveaways and Contests: Partner with influencers

to host giveaways or contests. These activities can boost engagement, increase followers, and generate excitement around your brand.

- Takeovers: Allow influencers to take over your social media accounts for a day. This can provide fresh content and attract the influencer's followers to your brand's channels.

Measure the success of your influencer partnerships by tracking key performance indicators (KPIs) such as engagement rates, reach, website traffic, and conversions. Use tracking links, promo codes, and analytics tools to attribute results directly to the influencer campaign. Analyzing these metrics will help you understand the effectiveness of the collaboration and inform future influencer strategies.

Maintaining good relationships with influencers is crucial for long-term success. Show appreciation for their work, provide feedback, and stay in touch even after the campaign ends. Building strong, ongoing relationships can lead to more effective collaborations in the future.

influencer partnerships can significantly enhance your social media marketing efforts by leveraging the trust and influence that these individuals have built with their followers.

5.5 Engaging Through Live Content and Webinars

Engaging through live content and webinars has become an increasingly popular and effective strategy for brands to connect with their audience in real-time. Live content, such as live streaming and webinars, offers a unique opportunity to interact directly with your audience, answer questions, and provide valuable insights and experiences that can't be replicated through static content.

Live Streaming: Live streaming on platforms like Facebook Live, Instagram Live, YouTube Live, and LinkedIn Live allows brands to broadcast content in real-time, creating an immediate and personal connection with viewers. Live streams can be used for a variety of purposes, including product launches, behind-the-scenes tours, Q&A sessions, interviews, and live events.

- Creating Live Content: Plan your live content around topics that are relevant and interesting to your audience. Promote your live sessions in advance through your social media channels, email newsletters, and website to build anticipation and ensure a good turnout. During the live session, engage with your audience by responding to comments and questions in real-time. Use interactive features like polls, quizzes, and shout-outs to keep viewers engaged and make the experience interactive.

- Technical Considerations: Ensure you have a stable internet connection, good lighting, and clear audio to provide a professional and enjoyable viewing experience. Test your setup before going live to avoid technical issues during the broadcast.

Webinars: Webinars are structured, online seminars that provide in-depth information and insights on specific topics. They are particularly effective for B2B marketing, education, and thought leadership. Webinars allow you to showcase your expertise, engage with your audience on a deeper level, and generate leads.

- Planning Webinars: Choose topics that address the needs and interests of your target audience. Webinars should be informative, engaging, and provide actionable takeaways. Collaborate with industry experts or influencers to add credibility and attract a larger audience. Promote your webinars through social media, email campaigns, and partnerships to maximize attendance.

- Engaging During Webinars: Use interactive elements such as Q&A sessions, polls, and chat functions to engage with attendees. Encourage participants to ask questions and share their thoughts throughout the webinar. Providing downloadable resources, such as slide decks or eBooks, can add value and keep your audience engaged even after the webinar ends.

- Follow-Up: After the webinar, follow up with attendees

by sending thank-you emails, recording links, and additional resources. This keeps the conversation going and provides further value to your audience. Use the opportunity to gather feedback and insights that can help improve future webinars.

Benefits of Live Content and Webinars: Live content and webinars offer several benefits, including:

- Real-Time Interaction: Engaging with your audience in real-time creates a more personal and immediate connection, fostering a sense of community and loyalty.
- Authenticity: Live content is perceived as more authentic and transparent, building trust with your audience.
- Immediate Feedback: Direct interaction allows you to receive immediate feedback, answer questions, and address concerns on the spot.
- Lead Generation: Webinars are effective tools for capturing leads, as attendees often need to register, providing you with valuable contact information.

Measuring Success: Track the performance of your live content and webinars by monitoring metrics such as viewership numbers, engagement rates, attendee feedback, and lead generation. Use analytics tools provided by the platform or third-party software to gather insights and measure the success of your sessions. Analyzing these metrics will help you refine your strategy and improve future live content and webinars.

engaging through live content and webinars offers a dynamic way to connect with your audience, provide valuable insights, and build a loyal community.

5.6 Creating Shareable Content

Creating shareable content is key to expanding your reach and fostering engagement on social media. Shareable content not only attracts likes and comments but also encourages your audience to spread your message within their own networks, amplifying your brand's visibility. To create content that resonates and gets shared, consider the following strategies.

Understand Your Audience: The first step in creating shareable content is to understand your audience's preferences, interests, and behaviors. Use analytics tools to gather insights into what types of content perform best with your audience. Consider demographics, psychographics, and past engagement patterns to tailor your content to their preferences. Content that speaks directly to your audience's interests and needs is more likely to be shared.

Craft Compelling Headlines and Visuals: Headlines and visuals are the first things people notice, so they must be attention-grabbing and compelling. Use strong, clear headlines that evoke curiosity or emotion. Pair your headlines with high-quality visuals, such as eye-catching images, videos, or infographics. Visual content is more engaging and shareable than text alone. For example, a travel company might use stunning photos of destinations paired with a headline like, "Discover the Hidden Gems of Bali."

Provide Value and Relevance: Content that provides value to your audience is more likely to be shared. This could be in the form of educational information, practical tips, entertaining stories, or inspirational messages. Ensure your content is relevant to current trends and events, as timely content can tap into ongoing conversations and increase its shareability. For instance, a fitness brand might share a workout routine that aligns with a popular fitness challenge or trend.

Incorporate Emotion: Emotionally charged content tends to be more shareable. Content that evokes strong emotions, such as happiness, surprise, awe, or even anger, can prompt people to share with their friends and followers. Use storytelling techniques to create an emotional connection with your audience. Personal stories, testimonials, and user-generated content can be particularly effective in evoking emotions and encouraging shares.

Use Interactive and Engaging Formats: Interactive content, such as quizzes, polls, and contests, can boost engagement and shareability. These formats encourage users to participate and share their results with their networks. Additionally, content that invites users to comment, tag friends, or share their own experiences can drive more interaction. For example, a food brand might run a recipe contest asking followers to share their unique dishes using a specific ingredient.

Optimize for Each Platform: Different social media platforms have unique characteristics and audience behaviors. Tailor your content to fit the format and style of each platform. For instance, short, catchy videos work well on TikTok, while in-depth articles and professional content are better suited for LinkedIn.

Incorporate Call-to-Actions (CTAs): Encourage your audience to share your content by including clear and compelling CTAs. Phrases like "Share this with your friends," "Tag someone who needs to see this," or "Retweet if you agree" can prompt users to take action. Make sharing easy by adding social sharing buttons to your content.

Leverage User-Generated Content: Featuring content created by your audience not only fosters engagement but also encourages others to share their own contributions. Highlighting user-generated content, such as photos, reviews, or testimonials, shows appreciation for your audience and builds a sense of community. This can lead to more shares as people are often proud to have their content featured by a brand.

Consistency and Timing: Consistently posting high-quality content keeps your audience engaged and increases the likelihood of shares. Additionally, consider the timing of your posts. Share content when your audience is most active to maximize visibility and engagement. Use analytics tools to determine the best times to post on each platform.

Monitor and Analyze Performance: Track the performance of your shareable content using analytics tools. Monitor metrics such as shares, likes, comments, and reach to understand what types of content resonate most with your audience. Use these insights to refine your content strategy and create more shareable content in the future.

creating shareable content involves understanding your audience, crafting compelling headlines and visuals, providing value, evoking emotions, and using interactive formats.

5.7 Measuring and Analyzing Engagement

Measuring and analyzing engagement is essential to understand how well your social media strategies are performing and to make data-driven decisions for future improvements.

Identify Key Engagement Metrics: The first step in measuring engagement is to identify the key metrics that matter most to your goals. Common engagement metrics include likes, comments, shares, retweets, and reactions. Additionally, consider tracking more nuanced metrics such as click-through rates (CTR), time spent on content, and video completion rates. Each metric provides a different insight into how your audience interacts with your content.

Use Analytics Tools: Leverage analytics tools provided by social media platforms, such as Facebook Insights, Twitter Analytics, Instagram Insights, LinkedIn Analytics, and YouTube Analytics. These tools offer detailed data on engagement metrics, audience demographics, and content performance. Third-party tools like Hootsuite, Buffer, and Sprout Social can provide a comprehensive view across multiple platforms and offer additional analytics capabilities.

Set Benchmarks and Goals: Establish benchmarks based on your current performance and set realistic goals for improvement. For instance, if your average engagement rate on Instagram is 3%, aim to increase it to 4% over the next quarter. Setting specific, measurable, achievable, relevant, and time-bound (SMART) goals helps you stay focused and track progress effectively.

Analyze Content Performance: Regularly review the performance of your individual posts and campaigns. Identify which types of content generate the most engagement and which fall flat. Look for patterns in successful posts, such as content format, topics, posting times, and visuals. For example, you might find that video content receives higher engagement than static images or that posts shared in the evening perform better.

Audience Insights: Understanding your audience is crucial for tailoring your content and engagement strategies. Use analytics tools to gather insights into your audience's demographics, interests, and behaviors. Analyzing this data can help you create more relevant and targeted content that resonates with your followers.

Track Conversions and ROI: Engagement metrics are valuable, but it's also important to track how engagement translates into business outcomes. Use conversion tracking to measure how social media interactions lead to actions such as website visits, sign-ups, purchases, or downloads. Calculating the return on investment (ROI) of your social media efforts helps you understand the financial impact and justify your marketing spend.

Monitor Competitors: Analyze the engagement metrics of your competitors to benchmark your performance and identify opportunities for improvement. Tools like Socialbakers and Sprout Social can provide competitive analysis and insights into industry trends. Observing what works well for competitors can inspire new ideas and strategies for your own campaigns.

A/B Testing: Conduct A/B testing to experiment with different content elements and strategies. Test variables such as headlines, images, CTAs, posting times, and content formats. Analyzing the results of A/B tests helps you determine what resonates best with your audience and refine your approach accordingly.

Adjust Strategies Based on Insights: Use the insights gained from your analytics to make data-driven adjustments to your social media strategies. If certain types of content consistently underperform, consider revising or eliminating them. Conversely, invest more resources into the content and strategies that drive high engagement. Continuously iterating and optimizing your approach based on data ensures that your social media efforts remain effective and aligned with your goals.

Report and Communicate Findings: Regularly report your findings to stakeholders, highlighting key metrics, insights, and recommendations. Use visual aids like charts and graphs to clearly communicate your performance and progress. Transparent reporting fosters a data-driven culture and helps align your team on strategic priorities.

measuring and analyzing engagement is a critical component of a successful social media strategy.

5.8 Responding to Feedback and Handling Negative Comments

Responding to feedback and handling negative comments is an essential aspect of maintaining a positive brand image and fostering a loyal community on social media. Constructive engagement with your audience, whether the feedback is positive or negative, demonstrates that you value their opinions and are committed to providing excellent customer service.

Acknowledge All Feedback: Start by acknowledging all feedback, whether it's praise, constructive criticism, or a complaint. Responding promptly and sincerely shows that you appreciate your audience's input. For positive feedback, thank the user and share your appreciation for their support. For example, a simple "Thank you for your kind words! We're thrilled you had a great experience" can go a long way.

Stay Calm and Professional: When handling negative comments or complaints, it's crucial to stay calm and professional. Negative feedback can be emotionally charged, but responding defensively or dismissively can escalate the situation. Take a deep breath and approach each comment with a problem-solving mindset. Acknowledge the issue, express empathy, and provide a constructive response. For instance, "We're sorry to hear about your experience. Please send us a direct message so we can address this issue and make it right" shows that you care and are willing to take action.

Respond Publicly, Resolve Privately: Whenever possible, respond to negative comments publicly to show other followers that you are attentive and responsive. However, move the detailed resolution process to private messages or email to maintain privacy and address the issue more effectively. This approach helps to manage the situation without airing all the details publicly. For example, "We're sorry to hear about your issue. Please send us a private message with your order details, and we'll resolve this for you as soon as possible."

Turn Negative into Positive: Use negative feedback as an opportunity to turn a dissatisfied customer into a loyal one. Follow up to ensure the issue is resolved and the customer is satisfied. For instance, if a customer complains about a delayed shipment, you might expedite their order and offer a discount on their next purchase.

Learn from Feedback: Negative comments often contain valuable insights into areas where your business can improve. Analyze recurring issues and identify patterns that may indicate a need for changes in your products, services, or processes. Use this feedback to make informed decisions and enhance your offerings. Communicate these improvements to your audience to show that you listen and are committed to continuous improvement.

Encourage Positive Engagement: Foster a positive community by encouraging and amplifying positive engagement. Highlight positive comments, share customer success stories, and create opportunities for your audience to share their experiences. User-generated content, such as testimonials and reviews, can be showcased to reinforce positive sentiment and build a supportive community.

Create Guidelines for Response: Develop clear guidelines for responding to feedback and handling negative comments to ensure consistency and professionalism across your team. These guidelines should outline your brand's tone of voice, response times, escalation procedures, and how to handle different types of feedback. Training your team on these guidelines ensures that everyone is equipped to manage interactions effectively.

Monitor Mentions and Keywords: Use social listening tools to monitor mentions of your brand and relevant keywords across social media platforms. This proactive approach allows you to identify and respond to feedback quickly, even if it's not directly addressed to your official accounts. Tools like Hootsuite, Sprout Social, and Brandwatch can help you track and manage your online reputation.

Handle Trolls and Inappropriate Comments: While it's important to engage with genuine feedback, you may encounter trolls or inappropriate comments that don't warrant a detailed response. For these situations, it's best to remain calm and not engage. If a comment violates your community guidelines, you can remove it and, if necessary, block the user. Always prioritize maintaining a respectful and safe environment for your audience.

Showcase Transparency and Accountability: Being transparent and accountable in your responses builds trust and credibility. If a mistake has been made, acknowledge it openly and explain the steps you are taking to rectify it. Transparency demonstrates integrity and can turn a potentially negative situation into an opportunity to strengthen your relationship with your audience.

responding to feedback and handling negative comments effectively is crucial for maintaining a positive brand image and fostering a loyal community.

5.9 Encouraging and Facilitating Online Reviews

Encouraging and facilitating online reviews is a vital strategy for building trust, enhancing your brand's reputation, and driving customer engagement. Positive reviews can serve as powerful endorsements that influence potential customers' decisions. Here's how to effectively encourage and facilitate online reviews for your brand.

Provide Excellent Customer Service: The foundation of receiving positive reviews is offering outstanding products and exceptional customer service. Ensure your customers have a great experience with your brand, from the initial interaction to post-purchase support. Satisfied customers are more likely to leave positive reviews.

Ask for Reviews: Don't be afraid to ask your customers for reviews. After a purchase or a successful interaction, send a follow-up email thanking them for their business and politely requesting a review. Personalize your request to make it more genuine. For example, "We hope you're enjoying your new product! We'd love to hear your thoughts. Could you take a moment to leave us a review?"

Make It Easy: Simplify the review process to encourage more customers to participate. Provide direct links to your review pages on platforms like Google, Yelp, Facebook, and industry-specific sites. You can include these links in follow-up emails, on your website, and even on receipts or packaging inserts.

Offer Incentives: While you should never buy reviews, offering small incentives can encourage customers to share their feedback. These incentives could include discount codes, entry into a giveaway, or loyalty points. Make sure your offer is ethical and complies with the review platform's guidelines.

Engage with Reviews: Show your customers that you value their feedback by responding to reviews. Thank those who leave positive reviews and acknowledge their support. For negative reviews, respond professionally and constructively, addressing their concerns and offering to resolve any issues. This engagement demonstrates that you care about your customers and their experiences.

Leverage Social Media: Use your social media platforms to encourage reviews. Share customer testimonials and reviews on your social channels to highlight positive experiences. Occasionally post reminders asking your followers to leave reviews and include links to your review pages.

Feature Reviews on Your Website: Highlight positive reviews and testimonials on your website to showcase customer satisfaction. Create a dedicated testimonials page or feature reviews on your homepage and product pages. This not only builds trust with potential customers but also encourages current customers to share their experiences.

Follow Up with Customers: After a customer makes a purchase, follow up with them to ensure they are satisfied and to request a review. Timing is important; send your follow-up email or message a few days after the purchase when the excitement of the new product is still fresh.

Use Automated Tools: Implement automated tools and software to streamline the review request process. Many e-commerce platforms and customer relationship management (CRM) systems offer features that automatically send review requests to customers after a purchase.

Create Review Campaigns: Periodically run campaigns specifically aimed at generating reviews. These campaigns could involve highlighting the importance of customer feedback, sharing how reviews have helped improve your products or services, and encouraging your audience to contribute.

Educate Your Customers: Sometimes customers need a little guidance on how to leave a review. Provide clear instructions and tips on your website or in your follow-up emails. A step-by-step guide can remove any barriers that might prevent customers from leaving a review.

Monitor and Analyze Reviews: Regularly monitor and analyze the reviews you receive to gain insights into customer satisfaction and areas for improvement. Use this feedback to make informed decisions and enhance your products, services, and customer experience.

Show Appreciation: Always show appreciation to your customers for taking the time to leave a review. A simple thank you goes a long way in building customer loyalty and encouraging future engagement.

encouraging and facilitating online reviews involves providing excellent customer service, making it easy for customers to leave reviews, asking for feedback, offering ethical incentives, engaging with reviewers, leveraging social media, featuring reviews on your website, following up with customers, using automated tools, creating review campaigns, educating your customers, and monitoring and analyzing feedback.

CHAPTER 6: SOCIAL MEDIA ADVERTISING STRATEGIES

S ocial media advertising has revolutionized the way businesses connect with their target audiences online. Unlike organic social media efforts, which rely on unpaid content sharing, social media advertising involves paid promotions designed to reach specific demographics, increase brand visibility, and drive desired actions such as clicks, conversions, or engagement.

Role of Social Media Advertising: In today's digital landscape, social media platforms serve as powerful advertising channels due to their extensive user bases and sophisticated targeting capabilities. Advertising on platforms like Facebook, Instagram, Twitter, LinkedIn, and TikTok allows businesses to reach millions of users based on demographic data, interests, behaviors, and even location.

Types of Social Media Ads: Social media ads come in various formats tailored to different campaign objectives:

- Facebook and Instagram Ads: Include photo ads, video ads, carousel ads, and stories ads, each optimized for specific engagement goals.

- Twitter Ads: Promote tweets, profiles, trends, or promote accounts to grow followership.
- LinkedIn Ads: Target professionals based on job title, industry, and company size, ideal for B2B marketing and professional networking.
- TikTok Ads: Utilize short video content to engage with a younger audience through challenges, hashtag campaigns, and influencer partnerships.

Benefits of Social Media Advertising: Businesses benefit from social media advertising in several ways:

- Targeted Reach: Precise targeting options ensure ads reach the most relevant audience segments.
- Increased Brand Awareness: Boost visibility and recognition among potential customers.
- Enhanced Engagement: Encourage interaction through likes, comments, shares, and clicks.
- Lead Generation: Drive conversions with optimized ad formats that prompt users to take action.
- Measurable Results: Track ad performance with detailed analytics to refine strategies and maximize ROI.

Ad Placement and Budgeting: Effective social media advertising involves strategic ad placement and budget allocation. Understanding where and how to place ads ensures they appear in front of the right audience at the right time. Budgeting considerations include bid strategies, daily or lifetime budgets, and ad scheduling to optimize reach and efficiency.

The Evolution of Advertising: As digital advertising continues to evolve, trends such as native advertising, influencer collaborations, and augmented reality (AR) ads shape new opportunities for brands to engage audiences creatively. Understanding these trends and incorporating them into strategies ensures relevance and competitiveness in the digital marketplace.

Social media advertising represents a dynamic and essential

component of modern marketing strategies.

6.2 Setting Advertising Objectives

Setting clear and specific objectives is crucial for any successful social media advertising campaign. Objectives provide direction, define success metrics, and guide the overall strategy. Here are key steps to effectively set advertising objectives:

1. Define Specific Goals: Start by defining what you aim to achieve with your social media advertising campaign. Common objectives include increasing brand awareness, driving website traffic, generating leads, boosting sales, promoting app installs, or improving engagement metrics such as likes and comments.

2. Ensure Measurable Outcomes: Objectives should be measurable to track progress and evaluate campaign success. Use metrics like click-through rates (CTR), conversion rates, cost per acquisition (CPA), return on ad spend (ROAS), or engagement rates to quantify results.

3. Align with Business Goals: Link advertising objectives directly to broader business goals and marketing strategies. This alignment ensures that advertising efforts contribute to overarching business objectives, such as revenue growth, market expansion, or customer retention.

4. Set SMART Goals: Use the SMART framework to ensure your objectives are Specific, Measurable, Achievable, Relevant, and Time-bound. For example, "Increase website traffic by 20% within the next quarter through Facebook advertising campaigns targeting new demographics."

5. Consider Audience Targeting: Tailor objectives based on your target audience's characteristics, behaviors, and preferences. This customization helps create relevant campaigns that resonate with specific audience segments, enhancing campaign effectiveness.

6. Prioritize Key Performance Indicators (KPIs): Identify key performance indicators aligned with each objective to monitor progress and evaluate campaign performance. Select KPIs that

directly measure success against your defined objectives.

7. Account for Budget and Resources: Assess budgetary constraints and resource availability to ensure objectives are achievable within allocated resources. Aligning objectives with budgetary considerations helps optimize campaign efficiency and maximize return on investment (ROI).

8. Adaptability and Flexibility: Remain adaptable and flexible in setting objectives to accommodate changes in market conditions, consumer behavior, or campaign performance. Regularly review and adjust objectives based on real-time data and insights.

By setting clear and measurable advertising objectives, businesses can focus their efforts, optimize campaign performance, and achieve meaningful outcomes through social media advertising. These objectives serve as benchmarks for success and guide strategic decisions throughout the campaign lifecycle.

This section outlines the importance of setting advertising objectives and provides actionable steps to define and prioritize goals effectively. Let me know if there's anything specific you'd like to add or modify!

narrative paragraph format

6.3 Audience Segmentation and Targeting

Effective social media advertising hinges on understanding your audience and delivering tailored messages to the right people at the right time. Audience segmentation and targeting are fundamental strategies that maximize the relevance and impact of your campaigns.

Understanding Audience Segmentation: Audience segmentation involves dividing your target market into distinct groups based on shared characteristics such as demographics, interests, behaviors, and psychographics. Each segment represents a unique audience persona with specific preferences and needs.

Benefits of Audience Segmentation: By segmenting your audience, you can create personalized messages that resonate with different segments. This approach allows you to address specific pain points, highlight relevant benefits, and speak directly to the interests of each audience segment. For example, a clothing retailer may segment their audience into categories such as fashion enthusiasts, budget-conscious shoppers, and trend followers, tailoring ads accordingly.

Utilizing Social Media Insights: Social media platforms provide valuable insights into audience demographics, interests, and behaviors. Use analytics tools to gather data on your audience's age, gender, location, hobbies, online activities, and purchasing behavior. This information informs segmentation strategies and ensures targeted advertising efforts.

Segmentation Criteria: Determine segmentation criteria based on factors that impact purchasing decisions and engagement with your brand. Consider variables such as:

- Demographics: Age, gender, income, education level, occupation.
- Psychographics: Personality traits, values, attitudes, lifestyles.
- Behavioral Data: Purchase history, browsing behavior, interaction with previous ads.

Creating Targeted Campaigns: Once audience segments are identified, craft tailored advertising campaigns that speak directly to the interests and preferences of each segment. Develop unique messaging, visuals, and offers that resonate with the specific needs of different audience personas. For instance, a fitness brand might create separate campaigns targeting gym-goers interested in strength training, yoga enthusiasts, and outdoor runners.

Dynamic and Custom Audiences: Leverage dynamic audience creation features offered by social media platforms to refine targeting criteria in real-time based on user interactions and behaviors. Custom audience tools allow you to upload customer lists or target users who have engaged with your content, visited your website, or interacted with similar brands.

Optimizing Ad Relevance: Enhance ad relevance by continuously monitoring audience insights and campaign performance metrics. A/B testing different messaging variations and visuals within each audience segment helps identify which content resonates best with specific groups. Adjust targeting parameters based on performance data to optimize ad delivery and maximize engagement.

Measuring Segment Performance: Evaluate the effectiveness of audience segmentation by monitoring key performance indicators (KPIs) for each segment. Track metrics such as CTR, conversion rates, engagement levels, and return on ad spend (ROAS) to assess which segments deliver the highest ROI. Use these insights to refine segmentation strategies and allocate resources effectively.

Continuous Refinement: Social media audience segmentation is an iterative process that requires continuous refinement and adaptation. Stay agile in response to evolving market trends, consumer preferences, and platform algorithm changes. Regularly update audience profiles based on new data and insights to maintain relevance and effectiveness.

Effective audience segmentation and targeting are pivotal in optimizing social media advertising campaigns for maximum impact and ROI.

6.4 Choosing the Right Social Media Platforms

Selecting the appropriate social media platforms for your advertising campaigns is crucial for reaching your target audience effectively and achieving campaign objectives. Each platform offers unique features, demographics, and advertising options that cater to different business goals and audience preferences.

Platform Demographics and User Base: Begin by understanding the demographics and user base of each social media platform.

Platforms like Facebook, Instagram, Twitter, LinkedIn, TikTok, and Pinterest attract diverse audiences based on factors such as age, gender, location, interests, and professional affiliations. Choose platforms where your target audience is most active to maximize reach and engagement.

Alignment with Campaign Objectives: Align platform selection with your advertising objectives and overall marketing strategy. Consider whether your goal is to increase brand awareness, drive website traffic, generate leads, promote products or services, or engage with a specific community. Different platforms excel in different areas, so choose accordingly.

Advertising Options and Formats: Evaluate the advertising options and formats available on each platform. Facebook and Instagram, for example, offer photo ads, video ads, carousel ads, and stories ads, each suited to different engagement goals. LinkedIn specializes in B2B advertising with sponsored content, InMail, and dynamic ads. TikTok features engaging short-form video ads popular among younger demographics.

Audience Behavior and Engagement: Analyze audience behavior and engagement patterns on each platform. Consider how users interact with content, engage with ads, and participate in discussions. Platforms with high engagement rates and active user interactions provide fertile ground for promoting brand messages and driving conversions.

Platform-Specific Features: Leverage platform-specific features that enhance advertising effectiveness. Explore tools like Instagram Shopping for e-commerce, Twitter's trending hashtags for real-time engagement, LinkedIn's targeting options for professional networking, and TikTok's creative ad formats for viral marketing campaigns. Tailor your strategy to leverage these unique features.

Budget Allocation and ROI: Allocate your advertising budget based on platform performance metrics and anticipated return on investment (ROI). Evaluate factors such as cost per click

(CPC), cost per thousand impressions (CPM), conversion rates, and ad engagement metrics to optimize budget allocation across platforms. Prioritize platforms that deliver the best ROI for your specific objectives.

Testing and Optimization: Conduct A/B testing to compare the effectiveness of different platforms and ad formats. Test variables such as audience targeting criteria, ad creatives, messaging tones, and call-to-action (CTA) strategies to identify top-performing combinations. Continuously optimize campaigns based on performance data to maximize results.

Monitoring and Analytics: Monitor campaign performance and analyze key metrics provided by each platform's analytics tools. Track metrics such as reach, impressions, clicks, conversions, engagement rates, and ROI. Use these insights to refine targeting strategies, adjust ad spend, and improve overall campaign effectiveness over time.

Adaptability and Scalability: Remain adaptable to changes in platform algorithms, audience behaviors, and industry trends. Stay informed about new features, updates, and best practices to stay ahead of the competition. Scale successful campaigns by expanding reach, increasing budget, or testing new platforms based on performance data and business growth objectives.

Choosing the right social media platforms for your advertising campaigns involves strategic assessment of demographics, advertising options, engagement metrics, platform features, budget allocation, testing, optimization, analytics, and adaptability.

6.5 Creating Compelling Ad Creatives

The success of social media advertising campaigns heavily relies on the creatives used in your ads. Compelling ad creatives capture attention, convey brand messaging, and drive user engagement and conversions. Here's how to craft effective ad creatives for social media:

Understanding Ad Creative Elements: Effective ad creatives consist of several key elements:

- Visuals: High-quality images or videos that grab attention and visually represent your brand or product.
- Copy: Concise and compelling text that communicates your message clearly and persuasively.
- Call-to-Action (CTA): Direct prompts encouraging users to take specific actions, such as "Shop Now," "Learn More," or "Sign Up."
- Branding: Consistent use of brand colors, logos, and fonts to reinforce brand identity.

Tailoring Creatives to Platform: Adapt ad creatives to fit the format and audience behavior of each social media platform. For example:

- Facebook and Instagram: Use visually appealing images or videos that tell a story and resonate with users scrolling through their feeds.
- Twitter: Craft concise and impactful messages within character limits, complemented by engaging visuals or GIFs.
- LinkedIn: Focus on professional visuals and copy that resonate with a business-oriented audience, highlighting industry expertise or thought leadership.
- TikTok: Create short, attention-grabbing videos that align with trends and capture the platform's energetic and creative atmosphere.

Visual Storytelling: Utilize storytelling techniques to create narratives that captivate and connect with your audience emotionally. Showcase real-life scenarios, user testimonials, product demonstrations, or behind-the-scenes content to humanize your brand and build authenticity.

Highlight Unique Selling Proposition (USP): Clearly communicate what sets your product or service apart from competitors. Highlight key benefits, features, or promotions that appeal to your target audience's needs and desires.

A/B Testing: Experiment with different ad creatives to identify top performers. Test variations in visuals, copy, CTAs, and messaging tones to determine which combinations drive the highest engagement and conversion rates.

Mobile Optimization: Ensure ad creatives are optimized for mobile devices, as a significant portion of social media users access platforms via smartphones and tablets. Use vertical formats, clear visuals, and legible text to maximize impact on smaller screens.

Compliance and Guidelines: Adhere to platform-specific advertising guidelines and policies regarding content, imagery, and messaging. Ensure creatives comply with regulations to avoid ad rejection or account suspension.

Creative Refresh: Regularly update ad creatives to maintain audience interest and relevance. Introduce seasonal themes, promotions, or trending topics to keep content fresh and engaging.

Performance Monitoring: Monitor ad creative performance using analytics tools provided by social media platforms. Track metrics such as click-through rates, engagement rates, conversion rates, and ROI to assess effectiveness and inform future creative decisions.

By focusing on these elements and strategies, businesses can create compelling ad creatives that resonate with target audiences, drive engagement, and ultimately achieve advertising objectives on social media platforms.

This section outlines best practices for creating impactful ad creatives tailored to social media platforms, emphasizing visual storytelling, A/B testing, mobile optimization, compliance, and performance monitoring. Let me know if there's anything specific you'd like to add or modify!

6.6 Optimizing Ad Targeting and Placement

Effective social media advertising involves strategic targeting and placement to ensure ads reach the right audience in the most impactful way. Optimizing ad targeting and placement enhances campaign performance, increases engagement, and maximizes return on investment (ROI). Here's how to optimize ad targeting and placement on social media:

1. Audience Segmentation: Utilize audience segmentation to divide your target audience into distinct groups based on demographics, interests, behaviors, and psychographics. Tailor ad content and messaging to each segment's preferences and needs to increase relevance and engagement.

2. Custom Audiences: Create custom audiences using customer lists, website visitors, or engagement data to target users who have already interacted with your brand. Leverage retargeting strategies to re-engage users who have shown interest but haven't completed desired actions, such as making a purchase or signing up for a newsletter.

3. Lookalike Audiences: Expand reach by creating lookalike audiences that mirror the characteristics of your existing customer base. Platforms like Facebook and LinkedIn allow you to find new potential customers with similar traits and behaviors as your current audience, increasing the likelihood of conversions.

4. Behavioral Targeting: Target users based on their online behaviors, such as search history, content consumption, purchase intent, and social interactions. Use behavioral targeting to deliver personalized ads that align with users' interests and recent activities, increasing ad relevance and engagement.

5. Geographic Targeting: Specify ad delivery based on geographic location, including country, region, city, or proximity to physical stores. Geographic targeting ensures ads are shown to users in relevant locations, optimizing local marketing efforts and driving foot traffic to brick-and-mortar locations.

6. Device Targeting: Optimize ad delivery for specific devices, including desktop computers, smartphones, and tablets. Consider user behavior patterns and device preferences to tailor ad

formats, visuals, and CTAs for optimal viewing and interaction on different devices.

7. Placement Options: Evaluate placement options offered by social media platforms, including feed ads, stories ads, messenger ads, in-stream video ads, and sponsored content placements. Choose placements that align with campaign goals and audience behavior to maximize visibility and engagement.

8. Ad Scheduling: Schedule ad delivery during peak times when your target audience is most active and likely to engage. Use platform insights and analytics to identify optimal days and hours for ad placement, ensuring maximum reach and effectiveness.

9. Budget Optimization: Allocate budget strategically across targeted audiences and placements to maximize ad performance and ROI. Monitor ad spend and adjust budget allocation based on performance metrics such as CTR, conversion rates, and cost per acquisition (CPA).

10. Creative Testing: Continuously test ad creatives, messaging, and targeting criteria to identify top-performing combinations. Conduct A/B tests to compare different variables and optimize ad elements based on performance data and audience feedback.

11. Monitoring and Optimization: Monitor ad performance metrics in real-time and make data-driven adjustments to optimize targeting and placement strategies. Track key metrics such as reach, frequency, engagement rates, and ROI to assess campaign effectiveness and refine tactics accordingly.

12. Compliance and Best Practices: Adhere to platform-specific guidelines and advertising policies to ensure ad compliance and avoid account penalties or ad rejection. Stay informed about updates and best practices for ad targeting, placement, and optimization on each social media platform.

By implementing these strategies, businesses can effectively optimize ad targeting and placement on social media, reaching the right audience with personalized messages and driving desired actions and conversions.

This section provides a comprehensive guide to optimizing ad targeting and placement on social media platforms, emphasizing audience segmentation, custom audiences, lookalike audiences, behavioral targeting, geographic targeting, device targeting, placement options, ad scheduling, budget optimization, creative testing, monitoring, and compliance. Let me know if there's anything else you'd like to explore further or if you have specific modifications in mind!

Conclusion

Effective social media advertising is essential for modern businesses looking to connect with their target audience, drive engagement, and achieve marketing objectives. In this chapter, we explored various strategies and best practices to maximize the impact of social media advertising campaigns.

Key Takeaways:

1. Strategic Platform Selection: Choosing the right social media platforms based on audience demographics, advertising options, and engagement metrics is crucial. Each platform offers unique advantages that align with specific campaign objectives and target audience preferences.

2. Compelling Ad Creatives: Crafting visually appealing and persuasive ad creatives that resonate with your audience is vital. Visual storytelling, clear messaging, and strong calls-to-action (CTAs) enhance ad effectiveness and drive user engagement.

3. Optimized Targeting and Placement: Implementing advanced targeting techniques such as audience segmentation, custom audiences, and behavioral targeting allows businesses to deliver personalized

ads to the right users at the right time. Strategic ad placement across different placements and devices maximizes visibility and interaction opportunities.

4. Continuous Optimization and Testing: Regularly monitoring ad performance metrics and conducting A/B testing enable businesses to refine targeting strategies, optimize ad creatives, and allocate budget effectively. Continuous improvement based on data-driven insights enhances campaign efficiency and ROI.

5. Adherence to Guidelines and Compliance: Adhering to platform-specific advertising guidelines and best practices ensures ad compliance and minimizes the risk of ad rejection or account penalties. Staying informed about updates and regulations is essential for maintaining successful advertising campaigns.

effective social media advertising requires a combination of strategic planning, creative excellence, precise targeting, continuous optimization, and adherence to best practices.

CHAPTER 7:
SOCIAL LISTENING: UNDERSTANDING YOUR AUDIENCE

Social listening is a powerful strategy that allows businesses to gain valuable insights into audience perceptions, preferences, and behaviors by monitoring online conversations and engagements across social media platforms. Unlike traditional market research methods, which often rely on surveys and focus groups, social listening provides real-time data and qualitative insights directly from consumers' interactions on social media.

Importance of Social Listening

Understanding your audience is foundational to crafting effective marketing strategies and delivering personalized experiences. Social listening goes beyond monitoring brand mentions; it involves analyzing conversations related to industry trends, competitor activities, customer feedback, and emerging topics of interest. By actively listening to what customers are saying on social media, businesses can:

1. Gain Deeper Insights: Social listening allows businesses to

uncover valuable insights into customer sentiment, opinions, and perceptions towards their brand, products, and industry. These insights provide a nuanced understanding of customer preferences and pain points, informing product development, marketing campaigns, and customer service strategies.

2. Monitor Brand Reputation: Monitoring brand mentions and sentiment helps businesses maintain a positive brand reputation.

3. Identify Industry Trends: Social listening enables businesses to stay informed about emerging industry trends, consumer behavior shifts, and competitor activities.

4. Enhance Customer Service: Social media platforms serve as accessible channels for customers to seek support, ask questions, and provide feedback. Social listening allows businesses to respond promptly to customer inquiries, resolve issues efficiently, and deliver exceptional customer service experiences.

5. Inform Content Strategy: Insights from social listening inform content creation strategies by identifying relevant topics, popular discussions, and content formats that resonate with the target audience.

6. Support Crisis Management: During crises or reputation challenges, social listening provides early detection of negative sentiment or issues brewing online. Businesses can implement proactive strategies to manage crises effectively, mitigate brand damage, and restore trust among stakeholders.

7. Drive Marketing Effectiveness: Social listening data enhances marketing effectiveness by refining audience segmentation, optimizing targeting strategies, and crafting personalized campaigns.

Implementation of Social Listening

To implement effective social listening strategies, businesses can use social media monitoring tools and analytics platforms that provide real-time data, sentiment analysis, keyword tracking, and competitive benchmarking. Establishing clear objectives, defining key metrics, and integrating social listening insights into decision-making processes ensures actionable outcomes and continuous improvement in customer engagement and brand performance.

By leveraging social listening as a proactive approach to understanding audience insights and market dynamics, businesses can cultivate stronger relationships with customers, drive innovation, and achieve sustainable growth in today's competitive digital landscape.

7.2 Leveraging User-Generated Content (UGC) for Engagement

User-generated content (UGC) has become a valuable asset for businesses seeking to enhance engagement, build authenticity, and foster community on social media platforms. UGC refers to any form of content—such as photos, videos, reviews, testimonials, and social media posts—that is created and shared by users rather than brands or organizations themselves.

The Power of User-Generated Content

UGC holds significant influence over consumer purchasing decisions and brand perceptions. Leveraging UGC allows businesses to harness the creativity and advocacy of their customers to:

1. Build Trust and Authenticity: Consumers trust UGC more than branded content because it reflects real-life experiences and unbiased opinions.

2. Increase Engagement: UGC often generates higher levels of engagement compared to brand-generated content. Encouraging users to share their content related to the brand or product sparks conversations, drives likes, shares, comments, and increases overall interaction with the brand.

3. Enhance Social Proof: UGC serves as social proof that validates a brand's value and quality. Positive reviews, testimonials, and user experiences shared by real customers influence potential buyers and encourage them to engage with the brand or make a purchase.

4. Foster Community and Advocacy: UGC fosters a sense of community among customers who share common interests and experiences related to the brand. Encouraging user participation and featuring UGC on social media platforms strengthens brand loyalty and turns customers into brand advocates.

5. Cost-Effective Content Creation: Incorporating UGC into marketing strategies reduces the need for extensive content creation efforts and costs associated with producing original content. Instead, businesses can repurpose UGC across various marketing channels to amplify reach and engagement.

Strategies for Leveraging UGC

To effectively leverage UGC for engagement and brand growth, businesses can implement the following strategies:

1. Encourage User Participation: Prompt customers to create and share UGC by launching contests, challenges, or campaigns that incentivize participation. Provide clear guidelines and encourage creativity to inspire diverse and compelling content.

2. Showcase UGC Across Channels: Feature UGC prominently on social media profiles, websites, product pages, and marketing campaigns. Highlighting real customer stories and testimonials enhances brand credibility and encourages others to contribute their experiences.

3. Obtain Permissions: Seek permission from users before repurposing their content to ensure compliance with copyright laws and respect for user privacy. Establish clear guidelines for content usage and crediting contributors appropriately.

4. Monitor and Engage: Regularly monitor social media platforms and online channels for UGC related to the brand. Engage with users who share UGC by liking, commenting, or reposting their content to foster a sense of appreciation and community.

5. Measure Impact and ROI: Track metrics such as engagement rates, reach, conversion rates, and brand sentiment associated with UGC campaigns. Analyze the impact of UGC on brand

perception and customer acquisition to refine strategies and optimize future campaigns.

CONCLUSION

L everaging user-generated content as a strategic asset can significantly enhance engagement, authenticity, and community building on social media platforms. Social media has transformed the landscape of marketing, offering businesses unprecedented opportunities to connect, engage, and build relationships with their target audience on a global scale. Throughout this book, we've explored comprehensive strategies, best practices, and tactics to harness the full potential of social media marketing.

Key Learnings and Takeaways:

1. Strategic Planning and Goal Setting: Successful social media marketing begins with clear objectives, audience segmentation, and strategic planning aligned with overall business goals.

2. Content Creation and Curation: Compelling content lies at the heart of engaging social media marketing. From creating visually captivating posts to crafting informative articles and videos, content that resonates with the audience drives engagement, builds brand identity, and fosters community.

3. Audience Engagement and Community Building: Building meaningful relationships through active engagement, responding to feedback, and fostering community spirit are essential for cultivating brand

loyalty and advocacy. Social media platforms provide unique opportunities for direct interaction and customer empowerment.

4. Advertising and Promotion Strategies: Leveraging paid advertising, influencer partnerships, and targeted promotions amplifies reach and drives conversions. Strategic ad placement, compelling creatives, and continuous optimization are key to maximizing ROI and achieving marketing objectives.

5. Analytics, Monitoring, and Optimization: Data-driven decision-making is fundamental to refining strategies and maximizing performance.

6. Social Listening and User-Generated Content: Harnessing the power of social listening allows businesses to understand audience sentiments, identify trends, and manage brand reputation effectively. User-generated content enhances authenticity, fosters community, and amplifies brand advocacy through genuine customer stories and experiences.

7. Adaptability and Innovation: In the dynamic world of social media, staying adaptable to platform updates, emerging trends, and changing consumer behaviors is crucial. Innovating with new features, creative approaches, and responsive strategies ensures relevance and competitive advantage.

Looking Ahead

As social media continues to evolve, embracing innovation, creativity, and ethical practices will be pivotal for sustained success in digital marketing. Social media marketing isn't just about likes, shares, or clicks; it's about building lasting relationships, driving meaningful interactions, and creating value for customers.

ADDITIONAL RESOURCES

To further support your journey in mastering social media marketing, here are some valuable resources that provide deeper insights, tools, and up-to-date information:

Books

1. **"Jab, Jab, Jab, Right Hook" by Gary Vaynerchuk**
   An essential guide to creating social media content that resonates with your audience.

2. **"Influence: The Psychology of Persuasion" by Robert Cialdini**
   Understand the principles of influence and how they apply to social media marketing.

3. **"Contagious: How to Build Word of Mouth in the Digital Age" by Jonah Berger**
   Learn the science behind why certain content goes viral.

Websites and Blogs

1. **Social Media Examiner**
   www.socialmediaexaminer.com
   A leading resource for the latest trends, strategies, and tips in social media marketing.

2. **HubSpot Blog**
   blog.hubspot.com
   Offers comprehensive articles on social media strategies, tools, and case studies.

3. **Buffer Blog**
buffer.com/library
Provides actionable advice on social media marketing, along with insights on tools and analytics.

Online Courses

1. **Coursera – Social Media Marketing Specialization**
www.coursera.org/specializations/social-media-marketing
A series of courses from Northwestern University covering everything from strategy to analytics.

2. **Udemy – Social Media Marketing Mastery**
www.udemy.com/course/social-media-marketing-mastery-2019/
A comprehensive course that dives deep into various social media platforms and strategies.

3. **LinkedIn Learning – Social Media Marketing Foundations**
www.linkedin.com/learning/social-media-marketing-foundations-2
Learn the fundamentals of social media marketing from industry experts.

Tools

1. **Hootsuite**
www.hootsuite.com
Manage and schedule your social media posts across multiple platforms.

2. **Canva**
www.canva.com
Create visually appealing graphics and content for your social media channels.

3. **Google Analytics**
analytics.google.com
Track and analyze your social media traffic and

engagement.

Communities and Forums

1. **Reddit – r/socialmedia**
   www.reddit.com/r/socialmedia
   A community for discussing all things social media marketing, from strategies to industry news.

2. **Quora – Social Media Marketing Topic**
   www.quora.com/topic/Social-Media-Marketing
   Engage with experts and enthusiasts to get answers to your social media marketing questions.

3. **Facebook Groups – Social Media Marketing Community**
   Search for active groups on Facebook where professionals share tips, strategies, and support.

STEP-BY-STEP TUTORIAL FOR SOCIAL MEDIA MARKETING

Step 1: Define Your Goals

Before diving into social media marketing, it's crucial to establish clear and measurable goals. Your goals will guide your strategy and help you track your success.

- **Increase Brand Awareness:** Expand your reach and make more people aware of your brand.
- **Generate Leads:** Use social media to attract potential customers.
- **Boost Sales:** Drive more sales through targeted social media campaigns.
- **Enhance Customer Engagement:** Interact with your audience to build loyalty and trust.

Step 2: Identify Your Target Audience

Understanding your audience is key to effective social media marketing. Define who you want to reach based on demographics, interests, and online behavior.

- **Demographics:** Age, gender, location, income, education, etc.
- **Interests:** Hobbies, topics of interest, lifestyle, etc.
- **Online Behavior:** Which social platforms they use, how they interact with content, etc.

Step 3: Choose the Right Social Media Platforms

Not all social media platforms are created equal. Choose the platforms that best align with your target audience and goals.

- **Facebook:** Broad audience, good for both B2B and B2C.
- **Instagram:** Visual content, younger audience.
- **Twitter:** Real-time updates, good for news and customer service.
- **LinkedIn:** Professional networking, B2B marketing.
- **Pinterest:** Visual content, often used for DIY, fashion, food, etc.
- **TikTok:** Short-form video content, younger audience.

Step 4: Develop a Content Strategy

Create a content strategy that aligns with your goals and resonates with your audience.

- **Content Types:** Blog posts, images, videos, infographics, stories, live streams, etc.
- **Content Calendar:** Plan your content in advance to ensure consistency.
- **Themes and Topics:** Focus on themes that interest your audience and align with your brand.
- **Tone and Style:** Maintain a consistent voice and style across all platforms.

Step 5: Create Engaging Content

Craft content that is valuable, relevant, and engaging to your audience.

- **High-Quality Visuals:** Use appealing images and videos.
- **Captivating Headlines:** Grab attention with strong, clear headlines.
- **Call to Action:** Encourage your audience to take specific actions (e.g., like, share, comment).
- **Storytelling:** Tell stories that resonate with your audience and humanize your brand.

Step 6: Schedule and Post Content

Consistency is key in social media marketing. Use scheduling tools to plan and automate your posts.

- **Tools:** Hootsuite, Buffer, Later, etc.
- **Best Times to Post:** Analyze your audience's behavior to determine the optimal posting times.
- **Frequency:** Maintain a regular posting schedule to keep your audience engaged.

Step 7: Engage with Your Audience

Social media is a two-way street. Engage with your audience to build relationships and foster loyalty.

- **Respond to Comments:** Answer questions and acknowledge feedback.
- **Join Conversations:** Participate in relevant discussions and trends.
- **Host Q&A Sessions:** Engage directly with your audience through live sessions.

Step 8: Monitor and Analyze Performance

Track your performance to understand what's working and what needs improvement.

- **Metrics to Track:** Reach, engagement, click-through rate, conversions, etc.
- **Tools:** Google Analytics, Facebook Insights, Twitter Analytics, etc.
- **Adjust Strategy:** Use data insights to refine your content and strategy.

Step 9: Run Social Media Ads

Amplify your reach and achieve specific goals through paid social media advertising.

- **Ad Objectives:** Choose objectives that align with your goals (e.g., awareness, engagement, conversions).
- **Targeting:** Use advanced targeting options to reach your ideal audience.
- **Creative:** Design compelling ad creatives that capture

attention.

- **Budget:** Allocate your budget strategically to maximize ROI.

Step 10: Stay Updated and Adapt

The social media landscape is constantly evolving. Stay updated with the latest trends and adapt your strategy accordingly.

- **Follow Industry Leaders:** Keep an eye on thought leaders and influencers in social media marketing.
- **Continuous Learning:** Take courses, attend webinars, and read industry blogs.
- **Experiment and Innovate:** Don't be afraid to try new tactics and learn from your results.

www.ingramcontent.com/pod-product-compliance
Lightning Source LLC
Chambersburg PA
CBHW052321220526
45472CB00001B/220